AutoCAD®

In 7 Days

Mohammad Imtaar

Acknowledgments

I am thankful to my students who asked me such questions whose answers were very helpful to make this book more useful.

Available from Amazon.com, CreateSpace.com, and other retail outlets

https://www.createspace.com/6379131

Introduction

Do you want to make floor plans or other drawings in fast and easy way using Autodesk® AutoCAD® ? But you don't have any practical experience of using AutoCAD, then this book is for you. You will start from scratch and the book will guide you in step by step exercises to learn the commands and procedures. I have tried to include all the information needed to complete different exercises in the book. I hope you will not be stuck at any point and waste your time in searching Help, Internet or other books to work on the topics.

The book doesn't teach you lessons to remember or doesn't ask you questions to answer. From Day 1, you start with a simple exercise with some basic commands and each day you will work on more complex drawings. By the end of Day 7, you may feel that you have enough knowledge of AutoCAD to work on large 2D projects.

Download Folder:

You download the required files from CadBook folder at
https://drive.google.com/open?id=0B0ostAbVyHuYOXV2WFJlbEtUdG8
and save them on your hard disk.

How to use this book:

1. Install AutoCAD 2010 or later. Download files from Download Folder.
2. Work on **EACH** step. If you miss even a small step or work on a step in wrong way, you may get error on a later step.
3. Enter all numbers (distances, angles, number of repetitions etc.) **accurately**. One wrong entry can disturb the whole exercise.
4. If you do a step wrong, click on **Undo** or press **Ctrl Z**. If several steps are wrong, delete the wrong object (select it and press Delete) and draw it again.
5. When you finish an exercise following all the steps, see the figure only and try to make it again without reading the steps. Read only that step which you cannot remember.
6. Once you are able to make the exercise without reading the steps, practice to make it in as little time as possible to increase your speed and accuracy.
7. Complete the steps 6 & 7 on the same day.

E-mail for Suggestions:

bimbooktech@gmail.com

What you accomplish on each day:

Day 1

You explore the AutoCAD user interface. You open a new file and make initial settings before starting a new drawing. You learn how to draw with absolute and relative coordinates.

Day 2

You learn how to make rectangular array by distributing objects in rows and columns and polar array by distributing objects on a circle. You draw a pattern using both rectangular and polar arrays.

Day 3

You make a grid and draw objects by snapping to grid points.

Day 4

You learn different editing methods to increase the speed and accuracy of your drawing.

Day 5

You learn how to manage your drawing using layers. You add information to your drawing in the form of text and dimensions. You learn using blocks as reusable objects. You add hatch patterns to represents materials.

Day 6

You draw a house plan with walls, doors, windows, furniture and fixtures. You also print a simple plot of your plan.

Day 7

You draw typical floor plan of a multistory hotel. You use external references to manage a complex drawing efficiently. You plot the floor plan on a sheet with title block. You also learn how to plot different parts of a drawing with different scales on the same sheet.

Contents at a Glance

Contents

Day 1   Coordinates, Lines, Arcs

AutoCAD drawings consist of drawing elements such as Lines, Arcs etc. You specify points for drawing elements e.g. Start and End points for a line, Start – Center – End points for an arc, Center point and Radius for a circle etc. The points are located on a coordinate system. You can specify points as Absolute Coordinates or Relative Coordinates.

But before starting a new drawing, you need to make some initial settings.

1.1 AutoCAD User Interface

When you start the AutoCAD program, what you see on the desktop is the user interface. Different tools are arranged in the form of a Ribbon. The default user interface shows the Ribbon and a large drawing area where you draw different elements of your AutoCAD drawing. (Fig. 1.1)

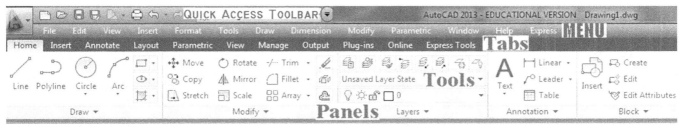

[−][Top][2D Wireframe]

Drawing Area

Fig. 1.1 – AutoCAD User Interface

1. The Ribbon consists of Tabs, Panels, Tools etc.
2. Each **TAB** (Home, Insert, Annotate, Layout ...) represents a particular topic.
3. When you press a tab, all panels change according to the topic of the tab.
4. Each panel contains tools to do a particular job.
5. On the top, you see Quick Access Toolbar (QAT). You keep frequently used tools on it. You can customize it by clicking on the dropdown arrow at the end of QAT.
6. A **contextual tab** appears to show tools to edit/modify a particular object. When job is done, the contextual tab disappears.
7. In the drawing area, you sketch/modify different AutoCAD elements.
8. The MENU is not shown by default. To show the menu, bring the cursor in the drawing area and type MENUBAR ↵ 1 ↵ (Fig. 1.2).
9. **Note: ↵ means press Enter key**.

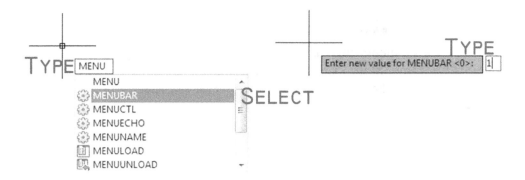

Fig. 1.2 – Show Menu

1.2 Status Bar

Status bar is located at the bottom of the AutoCAD window. It contains various tools to control different drawing aids.

1. These tools can be toggled ON or OFF by clicking on them or by pressing a function key.
2. If a tool is ON, it is displayed in blue color.
3. If a tool is OFF, it is displayed in grey color.
4. Some tools on the status bar are shown in Fig. 1.3. Their location or icon may be different in different versions of AutoCAD, but their function and related function key is same.

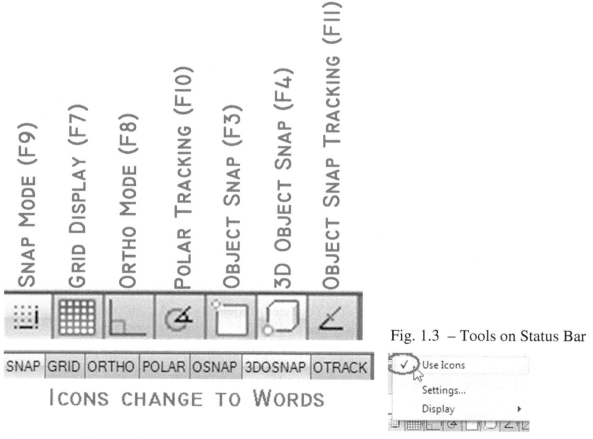

Fig. 1.3 – Tools on Status Bar

Fig. 1.4 – Change Icons on the Status Bar

5. If the icons seem confusing to you, you can convert them into word. Just right-click on any icon and unselect Use Icons. (Fig. 1.4). This feature is available in AutoCAD 2014 and before.
6. You also see Settings… in Fig. 1.4. If you click on Settings…, a dialog box will open to make different drafting settings (Fig. 1.5).
7. You can get Drafting Settings dialog box by clicking on Tools (on Menu) → Drafting Settings... (Fig. 1.6).

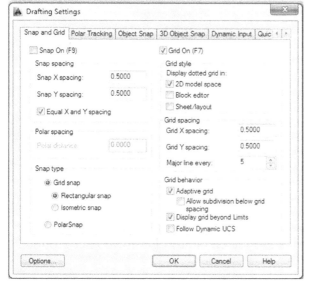

Fig. 1.5 – Drafting Settings Dialog

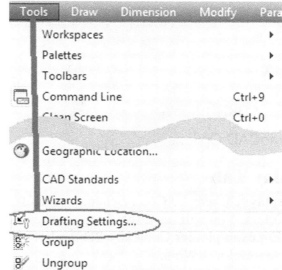

Fig. 1.6 – Drafting Settings Menu

1.3 Command Window

1. Below the drawing area, you see the command window (Fig. 1.7).
2. You can set its location.
3. You can adjust the width of previous commands.
4. You can see all previous commands in the text windows by pressing F2.
5. You can hide/unhide the command window by pressing Ctrl 9.

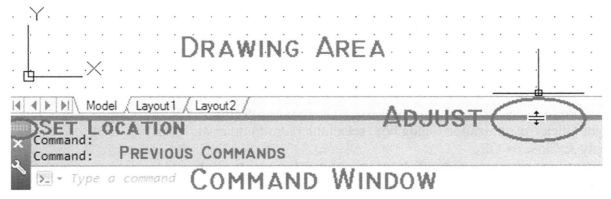

Fig. 1.7 – Command Window

1.4 Initial Settings

Before starting your first drawing, you may make some initial settings.

1. Click on AutoCAD button ![AutoCAD button] on the top left corner → Click Options (Fig. 1.8).

2. Alternatively, on the menu bar, click Tools → Options.

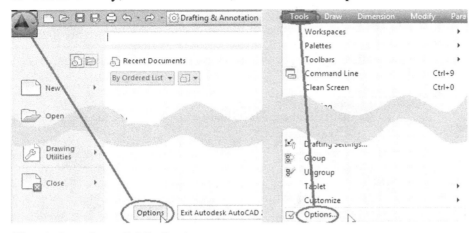

Fig. 1.8 – AutoCAD Options

1.4.1 Display Tab

1. On the Display tab, select a Color Scheme (Fig. 1.9).
2. Click on Colors. You will see a sub dialog box where you can select color of different Interface elements. For example, for Context = 2D model space → Interface element = Uniform background, you can select Color = White.

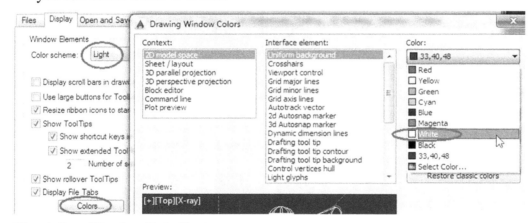

Fig. 1.9 – Display Tab Options

1.4.2 User Preferences Tab

1. On the User Preferences tab, click on Right-Click Customization (Fig. 1.10).
2. In the Right-Click Customization dialog box, select the radio-buttons shown in Fig. 1.10.
3. Click Apply & Close → OK.
4. After these settings, ↵ means right-click (or press Enter key). ↵ is used
   - to finish or end a command in progress
   - to finish the selection of objects
   - to repeat the last command

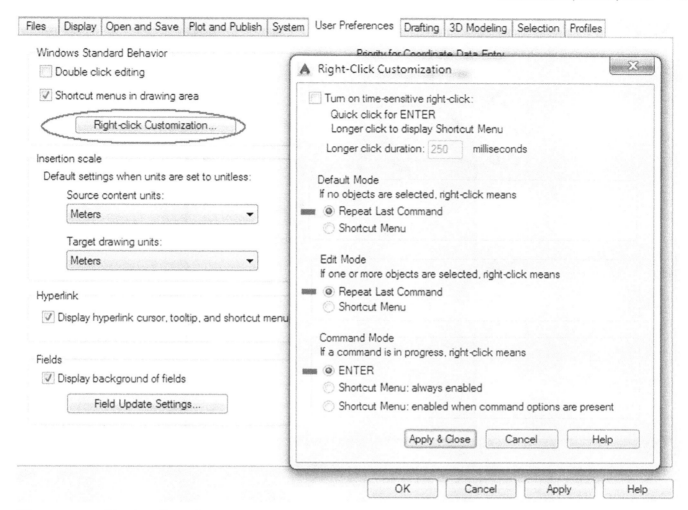

Fig. 1.10 – Display Tab Options

1.5 Absolute Cartesian Coordinates

Absolute Cartesian coordinates are distances from the origin (0,0,0) which is intersection of X,Y,Z axes. Look at the drawing shown in Fig. 1.11. Coordinates of all points are shown as absolute coordinates. The drawing consists of lines and arcs. First you will draw lines and then arcs.

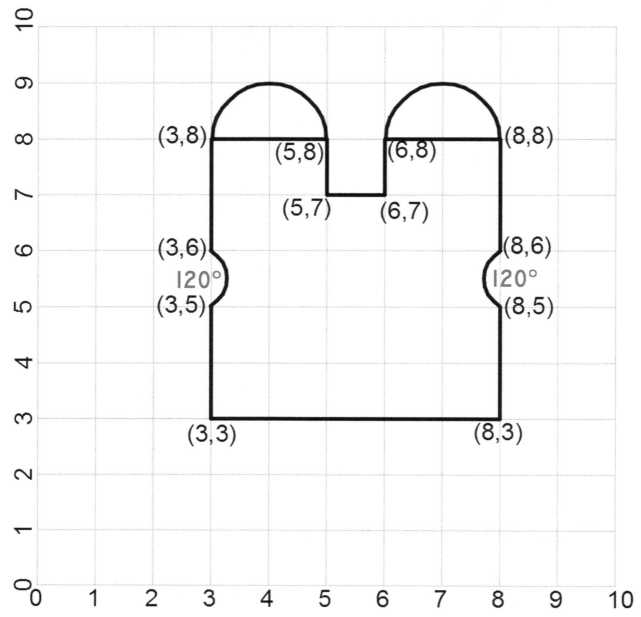

Fig. 1.11 – Drawing with Absolute Coordinates

1. Open (double-click on) Start.dwg found in CADFiles folder in Download Folder (page v)
2. Click on AutoCAD button ![icon] on the upper-left corner → Click on Save As → File name: **Ex01**.
3. As you can see from the drawing in Fig 1.11, the lower-left corner is at point (0,0) and the upper-right corner is at point (10,10). You will set these drawing limits for your AutoCAD drawing.
4. On Menu → Format → Drawing Limits
5. Prompt appears near the cursor. (**The prompt should appear near the cursor. If not then press F12 to turn Dynamic Input ON**).
6. To Specify lower left corner, type 0, 0 ↵
7. To Specify upper right corner, type 10, 10 ↵ (Fig. 1.12).
8. To adjust the screen for these drawing limits, you will select View → Zoom → All (Fig. 1.12) OR Type Z ↵ A↵ .

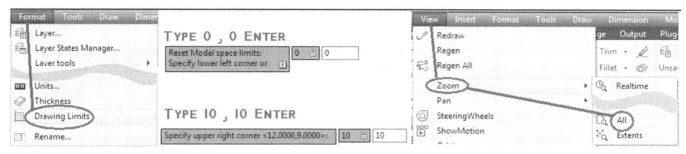

Fig. 1.12 – Set Drawing Limits

9. Now set the input for absolute coordinates. Tools → Drafting Settings → Dynamic Input tab → Pointer Input Settings → Select Absolute Coordinates (Fig. 1.13).

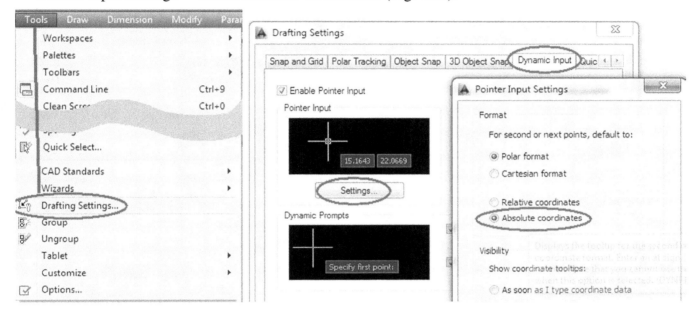

Fig. 1.13 – Input Absolute Coordinates

10. Now start drawing the line in the lower part of Fig. 1.10.
11. On Home tab → Draw panel → click on Line tool OR Type L↵ (Fig. 1.14).
12. Line command starts and prompts you to specify the first point. You type **3, 5**↵ . First point is placed on the screen.
13. Now you are prompted to specify the next point. You type **3, 3**↵ . First segment of the line is drawn.
14. In the same way you type **8, 3**↵ and then **8, 5**↵ .
15. To finish the line command, you press ↵ (Enter) again or right-click. Line command ends and you see the lower part of Fig. 1.10 drawn on the screen.
16. **Note: It is not necessary to select Absolute Coordinates in Fig. 1.13. If Relative Coordinates is selected in Drafting Settings, you can enter absolute coordinates by using #. For example, above line can be drawn by typing L↵ , #3, 5 ↵ , #3, 3↵ , #8, 3↵ , #8, 5↵ ↵**

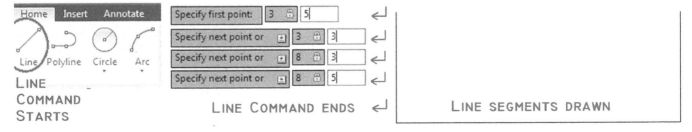

Fig. 1.14 – Drawing line segments

17. In the same way you will draw lines in the upper part of the drawing by starting the line command and typing **8 , 6**↵ and then **8 , 8**↵ and then **6 , 8**↵ and then **6 , 7**↵ and then **5 , 7**↵ and then **5 , 8**↵ and then **3 , 8**↵ and then **3 , 6**↵ . In the end right-click or ↵ (press Enter) to finish the line command.
18. If you feel that you have entered a wrong point, just type **U**↵ and enter the correct point.
19. Next you will draw arcs. The points are already there in the drawing so you don't need to enter any point. You will just snap to the points on the objects. You need to snap to Endpoints and Midpoints. Now you turn ON the snap to Endpoints and Midpoints.
20. Tools → Drafting Settings → Object Snap tab (or OSNAP → right-click → Settings) → Select Endpoint, Midpoint, Center (Fig. 1.15). Also turn on OSNAP by clicking on it or by pressing F3.

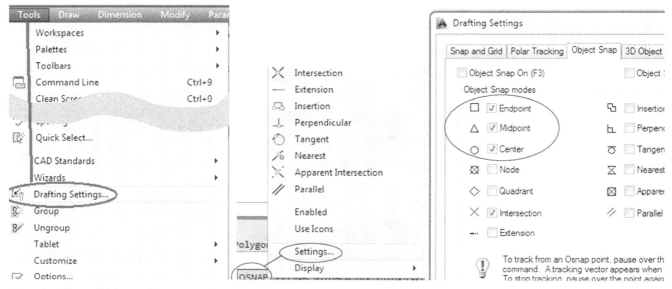

Fig. 1.15 – Object Snap settings

21. Arcs are drawn in ANTI-CLOCKWISE way. For the upper- right arc, start – center – end points are as shown in Fig. 1.16.

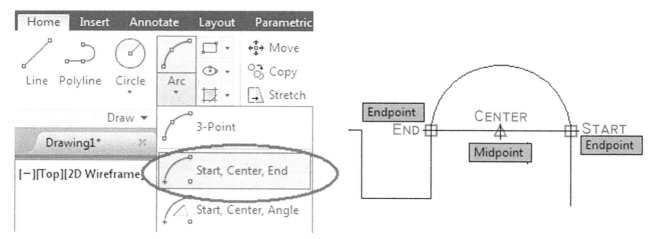

Fig. 1.16 – Draw Arc

22. On Home tab → Draw panel → click on dropdown arrow under Arc tool.
23. Select the option Start, Center, End (Fig 1.16).

24. Click near the points shown in Fig 1.16. Make sure you see the green Snap symbols as shown in Fig. 1.16.
25. In the same way, draw the upper- left arc.
26. For the middle arcs, Start – End – Angle are given.
27. On Home tab → Draw panel → click on dropdown arrow under Arc tool.
28. Select the option Start, End, Angle (Fig 1.17).
29. Click near the start point, then end point shown in Fig 1.17 and then type 120↵ (for the angle). Make sure you see the green Snap symbols.
30. For the other arc, repeat steps 23 – 25 above.
31. On Menu → Tools → Drafting Settings → Dynamic Input tab → Pointer Input Settings → Select Relative Coordinates (Fig. 1.13).

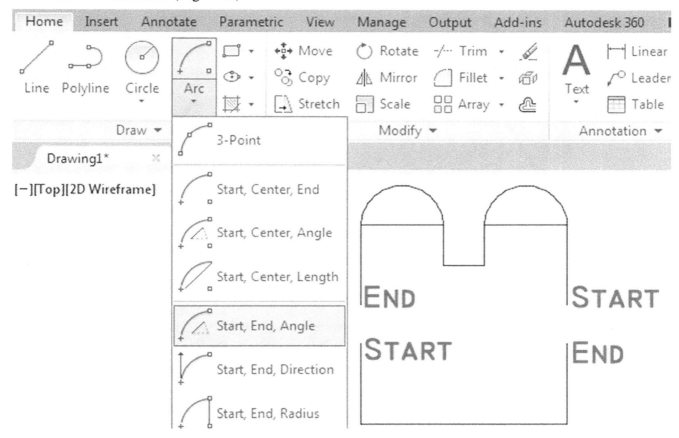

Fig. 1.17 – Draw Arc

32. Click 💾 on QAT (Quick Access Toolbar in Fig. 1.1) Or press Ctrl S to Save your work.

1.6 Relative Cartesian and Polar Coordinates

Relative Cartesian coordinates are distances from the last point you specified. Cartesian points are expressed in the form of (x, y) i.e., horizontal and vertical distance. Polar points are expressed in the form of (D, θ) i.e., distance and angle from positive x-axis.

Look at the drawing shown in Fig. 1.18. Coordinates of all points are shown as relative coordinates (Cartesian and Polar). The drawing consists of lines.

1. Open (double-click on) Start.dwg found in CADFiles folder in Download Folder (page v)

2. Click on AutoCAD button ⬛ on the upper-left corner → Click on Save As → File name: **Ex02**.
3. As you can see from the drawing in Fig 1.18, the width of the drawing is 14 and height of the drawing is about 10. You will set the drawing limits somewhat more than the width and height say 20, 15.
4. On Menu → Format → Drawing Limits → Type 0 , 0↵ 20 , 15↵ (Fig. 1.12).
5. To adjust the screen for these drawing limits, you will select View → Zoom → All (Fig. 1.12) OR Type Z ↵ A↵.
6. On Menu → Tools → Drafting Settings → Dynamic Input tab → Pointer Input Settings → Select Relative Coordinates (Fig. 1.13).

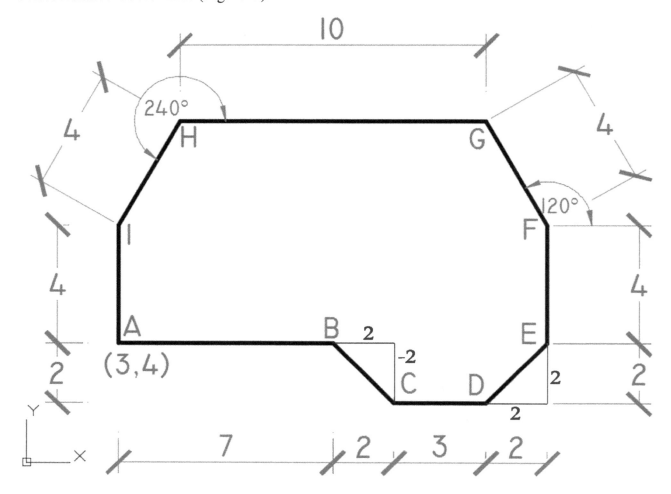

Fig. 1.18 – Relative Coordinates

7. On Home tab → Draw panel → click on Line tool OR Type L↵ (Fig. 1.14).
8. Line command starts and prompts you to specify the first point. You type **3 , 4**↵ . First point is specified on the screen.
9. In going from A to B, horizontal distance is x = 7 (right) and vertical distance is y = 0. You type **7 , 0**↵ . Line from A to B is drawn.
10. In going from B to C, horizontal distance is x = 2 (right) and vertical distance is y = –2 (down). You type **2 , –2**↵ . Line from B to C is drawn.
11. In going from C to D, horizontal distance is x = 3 (right) and vertical distance is y = 0. You type **3 , 0**↵ . Line from C to D is drawn.

12. In going from D to E, horizontal distance is x = 2 (right) and vertical distance is y = 2 (up). You type
2 , 2↵ . Line from D to E is drawn.
13. In going from E to F, horizontal distance is x = 0 and vertical distance is y = 4 (up). You type
0 , 4↵. Line from E to F is drawn.
14. In going from F to G, distance is d = 4 and angle is θ = 120° (relative polar coordinates). You type
4 < 120↵ . Line from F to G is drawn.
15. In going from G to H, horizontal distance is x = −10 (left) and vertical distance is y = 0. You type
-10 , 0↵ . Line from G to H is drawn.
16. In going from H to I, distance is d = 4 and angle is θ = 240° (relative polar coordinates). You type
4 < 240↵ . Line from H to I is drawn.
17. Bring cursor on A. When you see green square (snap to endpoint), click. Line from I to A is drawn.
18. Press Enter ↵ (or right-click) to end the line command.

19. Click  on QAT (Or press Ctrl S) to Save your work.

1.7 Ortho Mode and Tracking

When Ortho mode is ON (press F8), the cursor is restricted orthogonally i.e. the cursor will move horizontally (at 0°) or vertically (at 90°).

When Object Snap Tracking is ON (press F11), you can select a point along a path based on an object endpoint or midpoint or an intersection between objects.

Look at the drawing shown in Fig. 1.19. The drawing consists of lines and arcs.

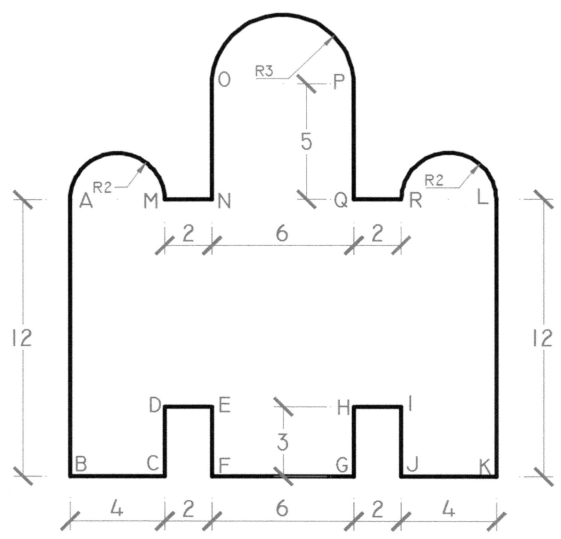

Fig. 1.19 – Ortho Mode - Tracking

1. Open (double-click on) Start.dwg found in CADFiles folder in Download Folder (page v)

2. Click on AutoCAD button [A] on the upper-left corner → Click on Save As → File name: **Ex03**.

3. As you can see from the drawing in Fig 1.19, the width of the drawing is 18 and height of the drawing is about 20. You will set the drawing limits somewhat more than the width and height say 25, 25.

4. On Menu → Format → Drawing Limits → Type 0 , 0↵ 25 , 25↵ (Fig. 1.12).

5. To adjust the screen for these drawing limits, you will select View → Zoom → All (Fig. 1.12) OR Type Z ↵ A↵ .

6. Turn Object Snap (OSNAP) ON. Turn Ortho Mode (ORTHO) ON. Turn Object Snap Tracking (OTRACK) ON (Fig. 1.3 – 1.4).

7. On Home tab → Draw panel → click on Line tool OR Type L↵ (Fig. 1.14).

8. Line command starts and prompts you to specify the first point. Bring cursor to left side of the screen where y ≈ 15 (Fig. 1.20 step 1) and click. Point A is specified.

9. Bring cursor down and Type **12**↵ (Fig. 1.20 step 2). Point B is specified.

10. Bring cursor to left and Type **4**↵ (Fig. 1.20 step 3). Point C is specified.

11. Bring cursor up and Type **3**↵ (Fig. 1.20 step 4). Point D is specified.

12. Bring cursor to left and Type **2**↵ (Fig. 1.20 step 5). Point E is specified.

13. Bring cursor down and Type **3** ↵ (Fig. 1.20 step 6). Point F is specified.
14. Bring cursor to left and Type **6** ↵ (Fig. 1.20 step 7). Point G is specified.

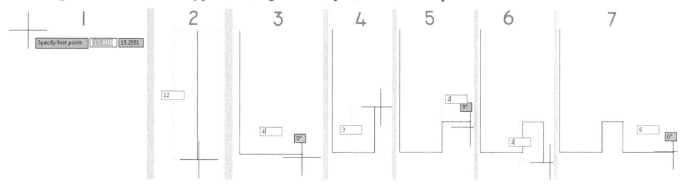

Fig. 1.20 – Steps using Ortho Mode

15. Bring cursor up and Type **3** ↵ (Fig. 1.21 step 8). Point H is specified.
16. Bring cursor to left and Type **2** ↵ (Fig. 1.21 step 9). Point I is specified.
17. Bring cursor down and Type **3** ↵ (Fig. 1.21 step 10). Point J is specified.
18. Bring cursor to left and Type **4** ↵ (Fig. 1.21 step 11). Point K is specified.
19. Bring cursor up and Type **12** ↵ (Fig. 1.21 step 12). Point L is specified.
20. Type **(Enter)** ↵ to finish the line command.

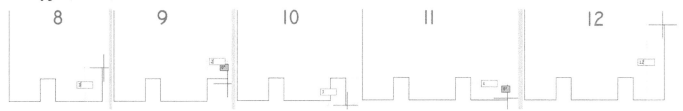

Fig. 1.21 – Steps using Ortho Mode

21. Click on Line tool OR Type L ↵ . Line command starts and prompts you to specify the first point.
    Bring cursor on point A. A green square appears indicating that the endpoint is snapped.
    DO NOT CLICK. Move cursor horizontally to left. A dotted green tracking line appears. Type **4** ↵
    (Fig. 1.22 step 13). Point M is specified.
22. Bring cursor to left and Type **2** ↵ (Fig. 1.22 step 14). Point N is specified.
23. Bring cursor up and Type **5** ↵ (Fig. 1.22 step 15). Point O is specified.
24. Type **(Enter)** ↵ to finish the line command.
25. Click on Line tool OR Type L ↵ . Line command starts and prompts you to specify the first point.
    Bring cursor on point O. A green square appears indicating that the endpoint is snapped.
    DO NOT CLICK. Move cursor horizontally to left. A dotted green tracking line appears. Type **6** ↵
    (Fig. 1.22 step 16). Point P is specified.
26. Bring cursor down and Type **5** ↵ (Fig. 1.22 step 17). Point Q is specified.
27. Bring cursor to left and Type **2** ↵ (Fig. 1.22 step 18). Point R is specified.
28. Type **(Enter)** ↵ to finish the line command.

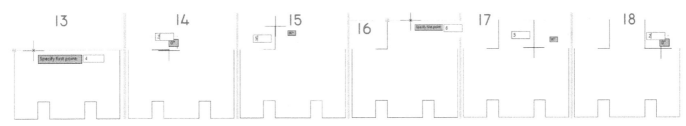

Fig. 1.22 – Steps using Ortho Mode with Object Tracking

29. Now you will draw arcs. On Home tab → Draw panel → click on dropdown arrow under Arc tool.

30. Select the option Start, End, Radius. Click near M, then A shown in Fig 1.23 and then type **2↵** (for the radius). Make sure you see the green Snap symbols.

31. Arc tool. Select the option Start, End, Radius. Click near P, then O shown in Fig 1.23 and then type **3↵** (for the radius). Make sure you see the green Snap symbols.

32. Arc tool. Select the option Start, End, Radius. Click near L, then R shown in Fig 1.23 and then type **2↵** (for the radius). Make sure you see the green Snap symbols.

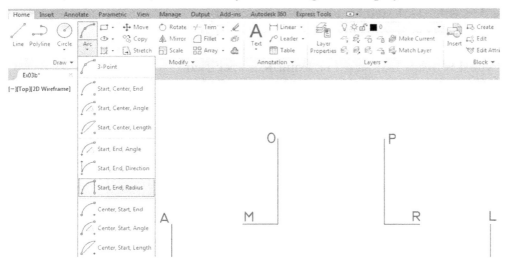

Fig. 1.23 – Draw Arcs

33. Click ![save icon] (Or press Ctrl S) to Save your work.

Day 2   Rectangular and Polar Array

Array command allows you to create copies of an object in a rectangular or circular pattern.

2.1 Rectangular Array

In rectangular array, objects are distributed in rows and columns (also levels for 3D). Look at Fig. 2.1.

There is a big rectangle starting at point A(0,0) with dimensions (235, 125).

There is a medium rectangle starting at point B(10,10) with dimensions (75, 105).

There is a small rectangle starting at point C(15,15) with dimensions (10, 15).

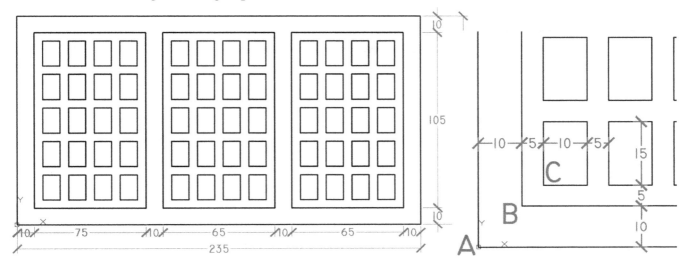

Fig. 2.1 – Rectangular Array

34. Open (double-click on) Start.dwg found in CADFiles folder in Download Folder (page v)

1. Click on AutoCAD button on the upper-left corner → Click on Save As → File name: **Ex04**.
2. As you can see from the drawing in Fig 2.1, the width of the drawing is 235 and height of the drawing is 105. You will set the drawing limits somewhat more than the width and height say 250, 150.
3. On Menu → Format → Drawing Limits → Type **0 , 0**↵ **250 , 150**↵ (Fig. 1.12).
4. To adjust the screen for these drawing limits, you will select View → Zoom → All (Fig. 1.12) OR Type Z ↵ A↵ .
5. On Home tab → Draw panel → click on Rectangle tool OR Type REC↵ (Fig. 2.2).
6. To draw a small rectangle, type **15 , 15**↵ **10 , 15** ↵ . A small rectangle is drawn.

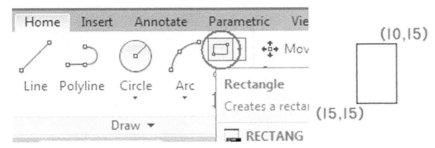

Fig. 2.2 – Draw rectangle

7. Next step is to repeat this rectangle in 4 (vertical) columns and 5 (horizontal) rows. The distance between the columns is 10 + 5 = 15 (distance from left to left OR right to right OR center to center). The distance between the rows is 15 + 5 = 20 (distance from bottom to bottom OR top to top OR center to center).

8. On Home tab → Modify panel → click on Array tool (Fig. 2.3). Prompt for Select objects appears. Click on the rectangle to select it. Press Enter ↵ or right-click to finish the prompt.

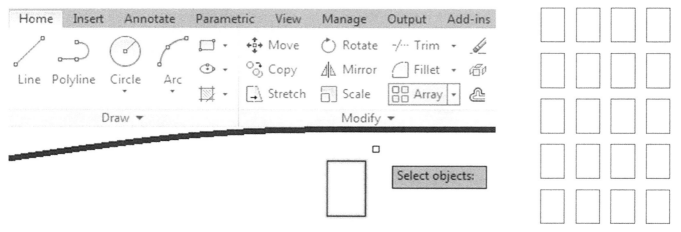

Fig. 2.3 – Array Command

9. Array Creation contextual tab appears. Make settings as shown in Fig. 2.4.

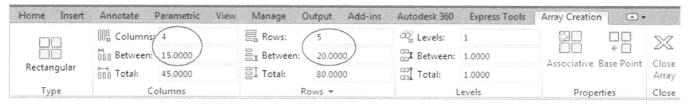

Fig. 2.4 – Array Creation contextual tab

10. Click on Close Array to finish the Array command. A 5 x 4 array of rectangles appear.
11. To draw medium rectangle, click on Rectangle tool OR Type REC ↵ . Then type **10 , 10** ↵ **65 , 105** ↵ . A medium rectangle is drawn.
12. This medium rectangle + 20 small rectangles are repeated 3 times horizontally (3 columns at a distance of 65+10=75 in 1 row only).

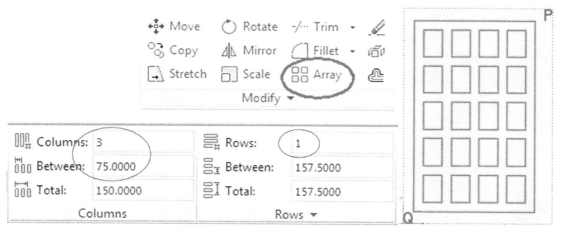

Fig. 2.5 – Rectangular Array

13. On Home tab → Modify panel → click on Array tool (Fig. 2.5). Prompt for Select objects appears. Make a selection window (Click somewhere outside on upper-right corner P then click somewhere outside on lower-left corner Q. All the objects inside the selection window (fully or partly) are selected. Press Enter ↵ or right-click to finish the prompt.
14. Array Creation contextual tab appears. Make settings as shown in Fig. 2.5.
15. Click on Close Array to finish the Array command. A 1 x 3 array appear.
16. To draw the big rectangle, click on Rectangle tool OR Type REC ↵ . Then type **0 , 0** ↵ **235 , 125** ↵ . The big rectangle is drawn.
17. The drawing shown in Fig. 2.1 is complete. Press Ctrl S to Save your work.

2.2 Polar Array

In polar array, objects are distributed on a circle.

Look at Fig. 2.6. In the lower-left part, a line is distributed on a circle. This is achieved by Polar Array command. This part is then repeated in 2 rows and 2 columns by Rectangular Array command. The upper-right part is scaled by a factor of 0.6 and the lower-right part is scaled by a factor of 1.4.

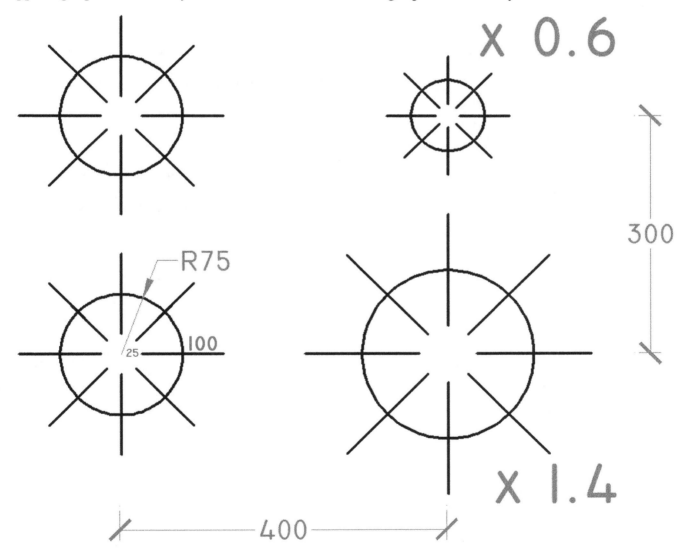

Fig. 2.6 – Polar Array

1. Open (double-click on) Start.dwg found in CADFiles folder in Download Folder (page v)

2. Click on AutoCAD button on the upper-left corner → Click on Save As → File name: **Ex05**.
3. As you can see from the drawing in Fig 2.6, the width of the drawing is about 500 and height of the drawing is about 400. You will set the drawing limits somewhat more than the width and height say 600, 500.
4. On Menu → Format → Drawing Limits → Type **0 , 0** ↵ **600 , 500** ↵ (Fig. 1.12).
5. To adjust the screen for these drawing limits, you will select View → Zoom → All (Fig. 1.12) OR Type Z ↵ A↵ .
6. On Home tab → Draw panel → click on Circle tool OR Type C ↵ (Fig. 2.7).

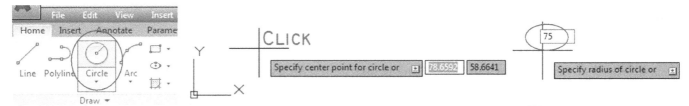

Fig. 2.7 – Draw Circle

7. You are prompted to Specify center point for circle. Click somewhere on lower-left side to specify center point for circle. Now you are prompted to Specify radius for circle. Type **75** ↵ . A circle is drawn.
8. Turn Object Snap (OSNAP) ON. Turn Ortho Mode (ORTHO) ON. Turn Object Snap Tracking (OTRACK) ON (Fig. 1.3 – 1.4).
9. Make Snap settings as shown in Fig. 1.15.
10. On Home tab → Draw panel → click on Line tool OR Type L ↵ (Fig. 1.14).
11. Line command starts and prompts you to specify the first point.
12. Bring cursor close to the circle and then to center of the circle. A green circular snap symbol appears. DO NOT CLICK. Move the cursor to right and type **25** ↵ .
13. Move the cursor to right and type **100** ↵ . Press Enter or right-click to finish the line command.
14. A line starting at 25 units to the right of the center and length = 100 units is drawn.

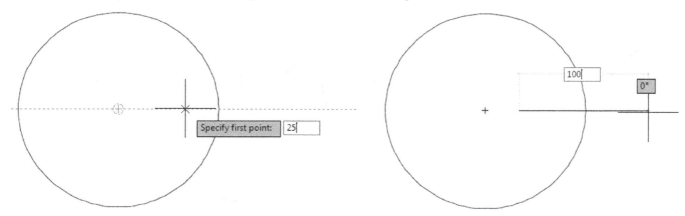

Fig. 2.8 – Draw Line

15. On Home tab → Modify panel → click on dropdown arrow to the right of Array tool and select Polar Array (Fig. 2.9). Prompt for Select objects appears. Click on the line to select it. Press Enter ↵ to finish the prompt.
16. You are prompted to Specify center point of array. Bring cursor near the center of circle. When you see a small green circle, click to snap to the center point of the circle.

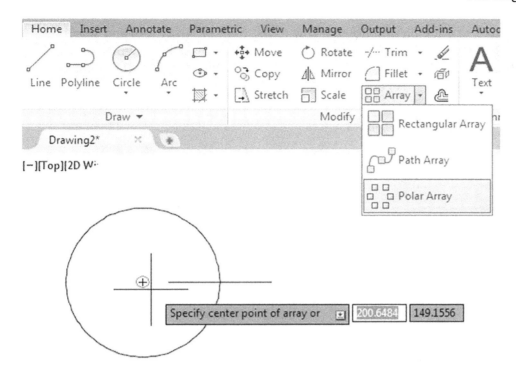

Fig. 2.9 – Polar Array

17. Array Creation contextual tab appears. Make settings as shown in Fig. 2.10.
18. Click on Close Array to finish the Array command. A polar array of lines appears.

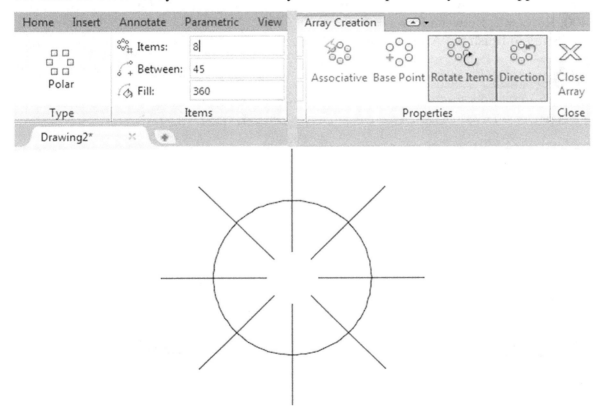

Fig. 2.10 – Polar Array Creation

19. On Home tab → Modify panel → click on dropdown arrow to the right of Array tool and select Rectangular Array (Fig. 2.11). Prompt for Select objects appears. Make a selection window (Click somewhere on upper-right corner A then click somewhere on lower-left corner B. All the objects inside the selection window (fully or partly) are selected. Press Enter ↵ to finish the prompt.

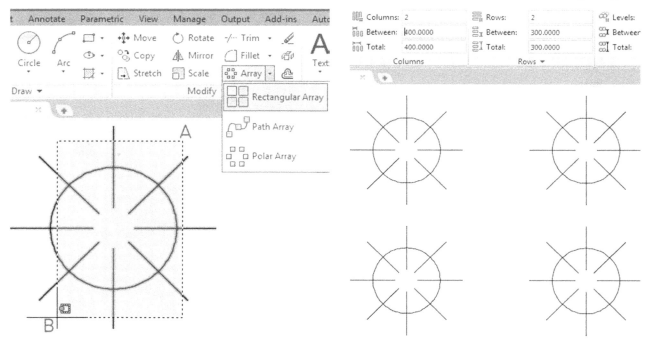

Fig. 2.11 – Rectangular Array Creation

20. Array Creation contextual tab appears. Make settings as shown in Fig. 2.11 (Columns = 2; Between Columns = 400; Rows = 2; Between Rows = 300).
21. Click on Close Array to finish the Array command. A 2 x 3 array appear.

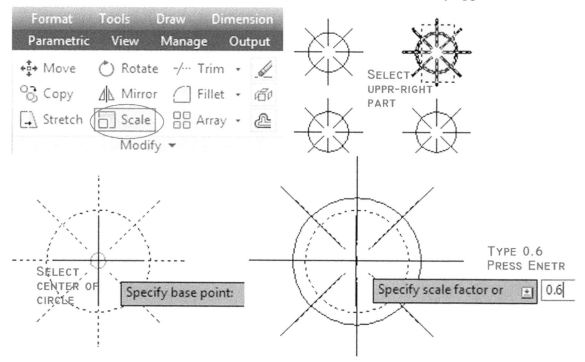

Fig. 2.12 – Rectangular Array Creation

22. On Home tab → Modify panel → click on Scale tool OR Type SC↵ (Fig. 2.12).
23. You are prompted to select objects. Select the upper-right part.
24. You are prompted to Specify base point. Snap to center of circle (click when small green circle appears).
25. You are prompted to Specify scale factor. Type 0.6↵ .
26. In the same way, scale lower-right part by a factor of 1.4.
27. The drawing shown in Fig. 2.6 is complete. Press Ctrl S to Save your work.

2.3 Pattern with Arrays

You can make interesting patterns using polar and rectangular arrays. One such example is shown in Fig. 2.13.

Fig. 2.13 – Pattern Creation using Arrays

1. Open (double-click on) Start.dwg found in CADFiles folder in Download Folder (page v)
2. Click on AutoCAD button ![A] on the upper-left corner → Click on Save As → File name: **Ex06**.
3. On Menu → Format → Drawing Limits → Type **0 , 0**↵ **10 , 10**↵ (Fig. 1.12).
4. To adjust the screen for these drawing limits, you will select View → Zoom → All (Fig. 1.12) OR Type Z ↵ A↵ .
5. Turn Object Snap (OSNAP) ON. Turn Object Snap Tracking (OTRACK) ON (Fig. 1.3 – 1.4).

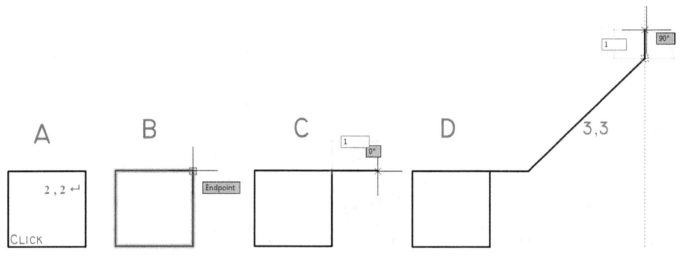

Fig. 2.14 – Rectangle and Line

6. On Home tab → Draw panel → click on Rectangle tool OR Type REC ↵ . Click somewhere on lower-left part of the drawing area, move cursor little away and type **2 , 2**↵ (Fig. 2.14 A).
7. On Home tab → Draw panel → click on Line tool OR Type L↵ . Snap to upper-right corner of the rectangle (Fig. 2.14 B).
8. Move cursor to right. When you see green dotted tracking line, type **1**↵ (Fig. 2.14 C).
9. Type **3, 3**↵ (Fig. 2.14 D).
10. Move cursor to up. When you see green dotted tracking line, type **1**↵ (Fig. 2.14 D).
11. Move cursor to left. When you see green dotted tracking line, type **1**↵ .
12. Type **-3, -3**↵
13. Click snapping to upper-right corner of the rectangle. You will get the drawing as shown in Fig. 2.15 A.

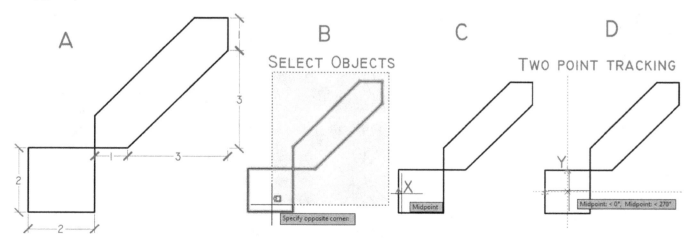

Fig. 2.15 – Two point tracking

14. Now you will make polar array of this drawing.
15. On Home tab → Modify panel → click on dropdown arrow to the right of Array tool and select Polar Array (Fig. 2.9). Prompt for Select objects appears. Select the drawing (Fig. 2.15 B). Press Enter ↵ to finish the prompt.
16. You are prompted to Specify center point of array which is center of the rectangle. You need tracking from mid-point of vertical side and mid-point of horizontal side.
17. Bring cursor on X (mid-point of vertical side. Fig. 2.15 C). You will see a small triangle (mid-point snap symbol). DO NOT CLICK. Move cursor to right. You will see green dotted horizontal tracking line.
18. Bring cursor on Y (mid-point of horizontal side. Fig. 2.15 D). You will see a small triangle (mid-point snap symbol). DO NOT CLICK. Move cursor down until you will see green dotted tracking lines from both mid-points. Now CLICK to track the middle point of the rectangle.

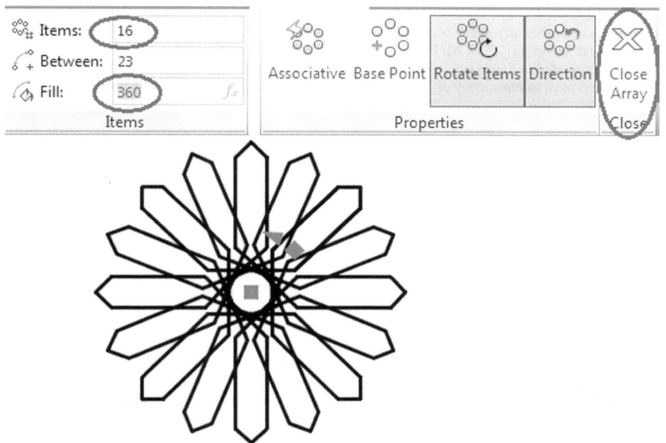

Fig. 2.16 – Two point tracking

19. Array Creation contextual tab appears. Make settings as shown in Fig. 2.16 (Items = 16, Fill = 360). Click Close Array.
20. **Rotate wheel of mouse to zoom in or out. Press wheel and drag to pan.**

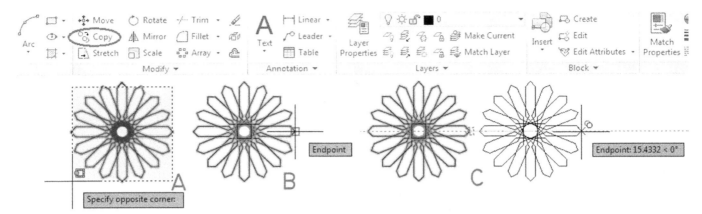

Fig. 2.17 – Copy Command

21. On Home tab → Modify panel → click on Copy tool (Fig. 2.17). Prompt for Select objects appears. Select the drawing (Fig. 2.17 A). Press Enter ↵ to finish the prompt.

22. You are prompted to Specify base point. Snap to middle-right point (Fig. 2.17 B). Move cursor away to right and click to make copy of the drawing (Fig. 2.17 C). Press **Enter or ESC** to finish the Copy command.

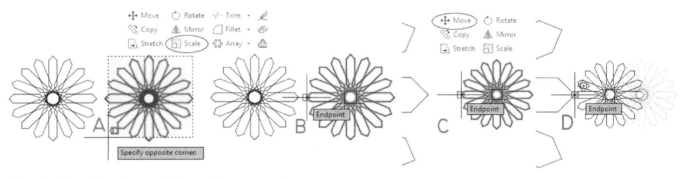

Fig. 2.18 – Scale and Move Commands

23. On Home tab → Modify panel → click on Scale tool OR Type SC ↵ .

24. You are prompted to select objects. Select the right copied part (Fig. 2.18 A).

25. You are prompted to Specify base point. Snap to middle-left point (click when small green square appears Fig. 2.18 B).

26. You are prompted to Specify scale factor. Type 0.2 ↵ . The right part is scaled down by a factor of 0.2.

27. On Home tab → Modify panel → click on Move tool OR Type M ↵ .

28. You are prompted to select objects. Select the right scaled part (Fig. 2.18 C).

29. You are prompted to Specify base point. Snap to middle-left point (click when small green square appears Fig. 2.17 C).

30. You are prompted to Specify second point. Snap to middle-right point of left part (Fig. 2.18 D). You will get a drawing as shown in Fig. 2.19 A.

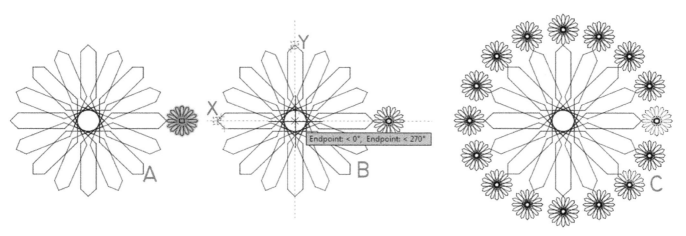

Fig. 2.19 – Polar Array with Two point Tracking

31. Now you will make polar array of the scaled part.
32. On Home tab → Modify panel → click on dropdown arrow to the right of Array tool and select Polar Array (Fig. 2.9). Prompt for Select objects appears. Select the right scaled part (Fig. 2.19 A). Press Enter ↵ to finish the prompt.
33. You are prompted to Specify center point of array which is center of the rectangle. You need 2 point tracking for middle point of the big drawing.
34. Bring cursor on X (middle-left point Fig. 2.19 B). You will see a small square (end-point snap symbol). DO NOT CLICK. Move cursor to right. You will see green dotted horizontal tracking line.
35. Bring cursor on Y (middle-top point Fig. 2.19 B). You will see a small square (end-point snap symbol). DO NOT CLICK. Move cursor down until you will see green dotted tracking lines from both end-points. Now CLICK to track the middle point of the drawing.
36. Array Creation contextual tab appears. Make settings as shown in Fig. 2.16. Click Close Array. You will get the drawing as shown in Fig. 2.19 C.

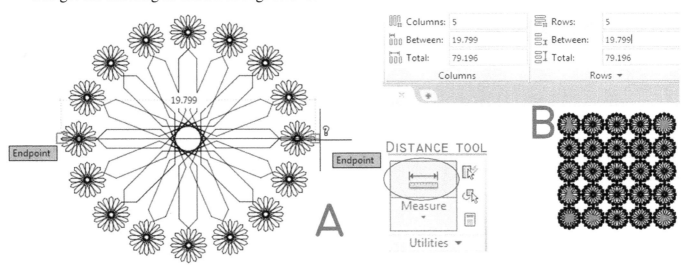

Fig. 2.20 – Rectangular Array

37. Now you will make a 5 x 5 rectangular array of the drawing. But you need to know the distance between columns and rows which is equal to the width of the drawing.
38. On Home tab → Utilities panel → click on Distance tool. Click on middle-left end-point and then middle-right end-point (Fig. 2.20 A). You will that the distance is 19.799.

39. On Home tab → Modify panel → click on dropdown arrow to the right of Array tool and select Rectangular Array (Fig. 2.11). Prompt for Select objects appears. Select the whole drawing. Press Enter ↵ to finish the prompt.
40. Array Creation contextual tab appears. Make settings as shown in Fig. 2.20 B (Columns = 5; Between Columns = 19.799; Rows = 5; Between Rows = 19.799).
41. Click on Close Array to finish the Array command. A 5 x 5 array appear.
42. The drawing shown in Fig. 2.13 is complete. Press Ctrl S to Save your work.

Day 3   Drawing on Grid

Sometimes you put a sheet of grid paper under the drawing to help you in adjusting distances and aligning objects. AutoCAD grid is a drawing aid for this purpose.

You can display the grid in the form of rectangular pattern of lines or dots.

You can turn the grid display ON or OFF by pressing F7 (Fig. 1.3 – 1.4).

You can turn the grid snap ON or OFF by pressing F9 (Fig. 1.3 – 1.4).

3.1 Grid Settings

Look at the drawing in Fig. 3.1. Grid is displayed in the form of points. Lines and arcs are drawn by snapping to grid points.

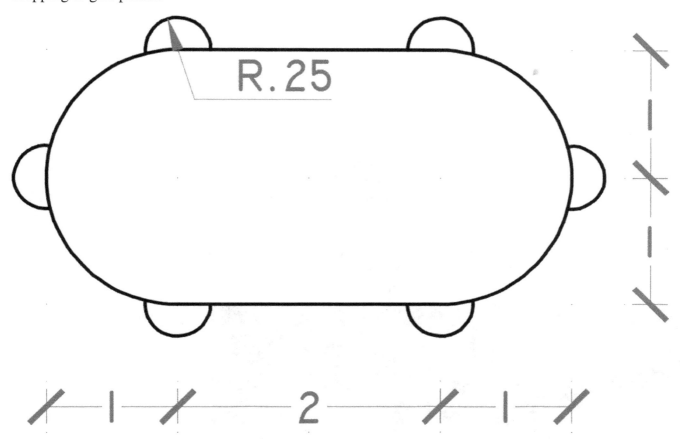

Fig. 3.1 – Grid Settings

1. Open (double-click on) Start.dwg found in CADFiles folder in Download Folder (page v)

2. Click on AutoCAD button ![A] on the upper-left corner → Click on Save As → File name: **Ex07**.
3. On Menu → Format → Drawing Limits → Type **0 , 0**↵ **7 , 5**↵ (Fig. 1.12).
4. To adjust the screen for these drawing limits, you will select View → Zoom → All (Fig. 1.12) OR Type Z ↵ A↵ .
5. Turn Object Snap (OSNAP) OFF (Fig. 1.3 – 1.4).

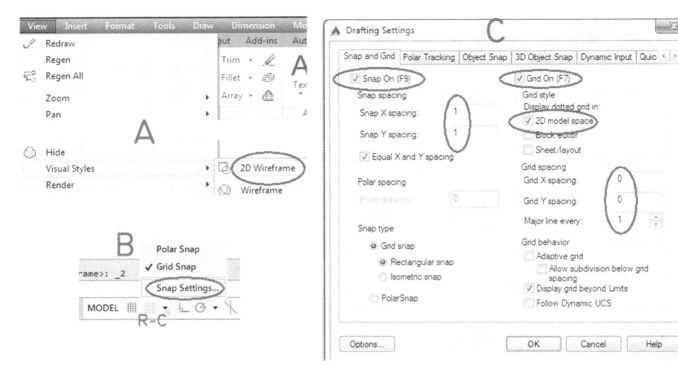

Fig. 3.2 – Grid Settings

6. On Menu → View → Visual Styles → 2D Wireframe (Fig. 3.2 A).
7. On Status Bar, right-click on Grid Display icon. Click on Snap Settings… (Fig. 3.2 B).
8. Drafting Settings dialog box appears. On Snap and grid tab, make settings as shown in (Fig. 3.2 C). Press OK. Grid dots appear on the screen. Horizontal and vertical distance between the dots is 1 unit.
9. On Home tab → Draw panel → click on Line tool OR Type L ↵ (Fig. 1.14).
10. Line command starts and prompts you to specify the first point. Click on dot A and then on B (2 units to right). Similarly draw a line from C to D (Fig. 3.3).
11. On Home tab → Draw panel → click on dropdown arrow under Arc tool.

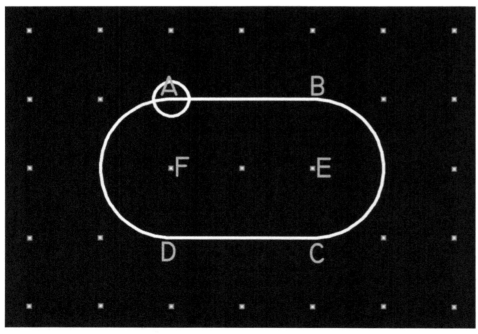

Fig. 3.3 – Draw on Grid

12. Select the option Start, Center, End (Fig 1.16).
13. Click on A – F – D to draw left side arc.
14. Click on C – E – B to draw right side arc.
15. On Home tab → Draw panel → click on Circle tool OR Type C ↵ .
16. You are prompted to Specify center point for circle. Click on A. Type **0.25** ↵ . A circle of radius = 0.25 is drawn.

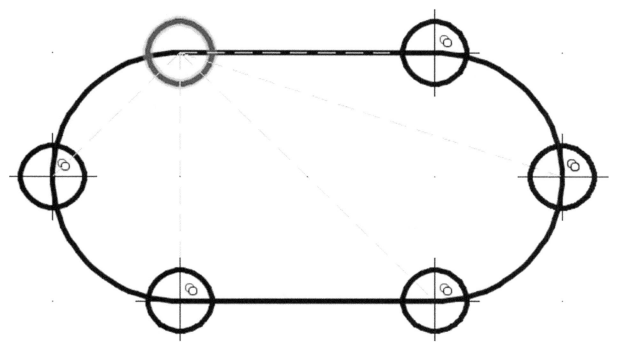

Fig. 3.4 – Copy Circles

17. On Home tab → Modify panel → click on Copy tool. Prompt for Select objects appears. Select the circle. Press Enter ↵ to finish the prompt.
18. You are prompted to Specify base point. Click on point A (center of circle).
19. Click on other points shown in Fig. 3.4 to copy circles. Press **Enter** or **ESC** or **right-click** to finish the Copy command.

Fig. 3.5 – Trim command

20. On Home tab → Modify panel → click on Trim tool. Prompt for Select objects appears. Select the two lines and two arcs (Fig 3.5). Press Enter ↵ to finish the prompt.
21. Prompt for Select objects to Trim appears. Click on inner sides of the circles. Press **Enter** or **ESC** or **right-click** to finish the Trim command.
22. The drawing shown in Fig. 3.1 is complete. Press Ctrl S to Save your work.

3.2 Extend Command on Grid

Look at the drawing in Fig. 3.6. Grid is displayed in the form of points. Lines and arcs are drawn by snapping to grid points.

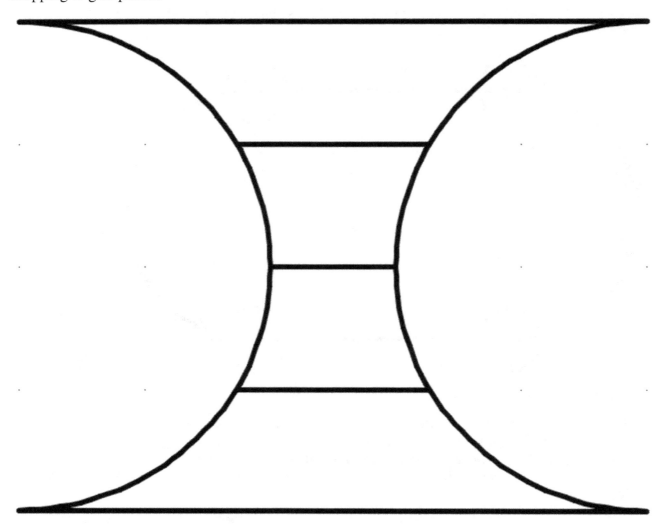

Fig. 3.6 – Extend command

1. Repeat steps 1 – 8 of § 3.1 Saving file As **Ex08**.
2. On Home tab → Draw panel → click on dropdown arrow under Arc tool.

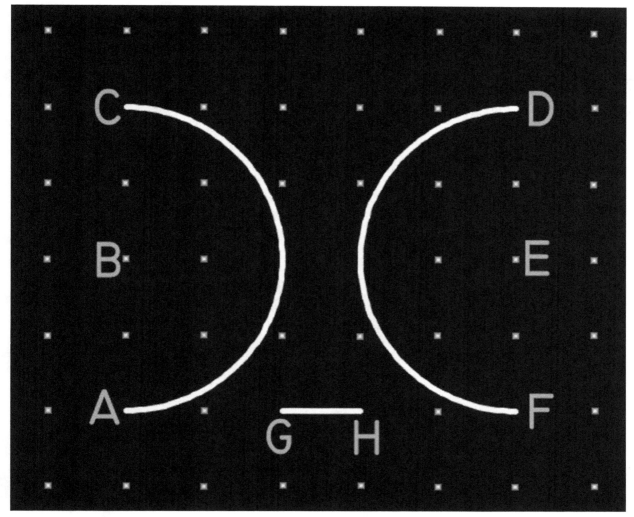

Fig. 3.7 – Line and Arcs on Grid

3. Select the option Start, Center, End (Fig 1.16).
4. Click on A – B – C to draw left side arc.
5. Click on D – E – F to draw right side arc.
6. Draw a line by clicking on G – H.
7. Make rectangular array for the line GH. (Columns = 1; Rows = 5; Between Rows = 1). You will get the drawing shown in Fig. 3.8 A.

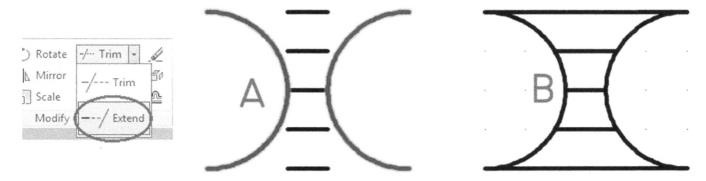

Fig. 3.8 – Extend command

8. On Home tab → Modify panel → click on dropdown arrow besides Trim tool and click on Extend tool. Prompt for Select objects appears. Select the two arcs (Fig 3.8 A). Press Enter↵ to finish the prompt.

9. Prompt for Select objects to Extend appears. Click on left and right sides of the lines. Press **Enter** or **ESC** to finish the Trim command.

10. The drawing shown in Fig. 3.6 is complete. Press Ctrl S to Save your work.

Day 4   Editing Techniques

You need to know some editing methods to increase the speed and accuracy of your drawing. You are already familiar with some of the methods such as Array, Copy, Trim, Extend etc. Today you will be introduced with more methods and commands.

4.1 Copy – Rotate – Move – Mirror

Look at the drawing in Fig. 4.1. You will use Copy – Rotate – Move – Mirror commands to complete it.

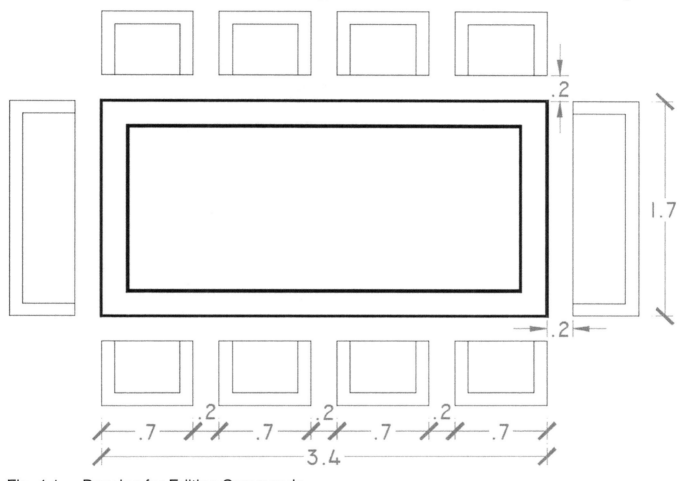

Fig. 4.1 – Drawing for Editing Commands

1. Open Start.dwg and Save As **Ex09**.
2. On Menu → Format → Drawing Limits → Type **0 , 0** ↵ **5 , 3** ↵ → Type Z ↵ A↵ .
3. Turn Object Snap (OSNAP) OFF.
4. In the Snap and Grid dialog box (Fig. 3.2 C) set Snap X Spacing = 0.1 and Snap Y Spacing = 0.1. Keep other settings same.
5. On Home tab → Draw panel → click on Rectangle tool OR Type REC ↵ . Click somewhere in lower-left side of the drawing area. Type **3.4 , 1.7** ↵ . A rectangle is drawn (Fig. 4.2).

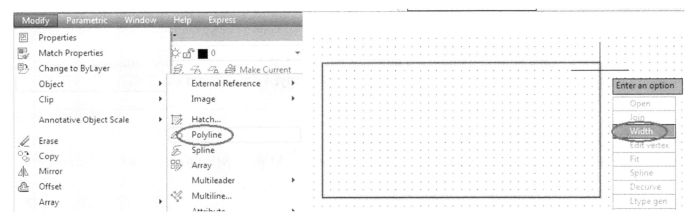

Fig. 4.2 – Edit Polyline

6. On Menu → Modify → Object → click Polyline OR Type PEDIT ↵ .
7. Select the rectangle → click on Width → type 0.02 ↵ . The rectangle becomes thick.

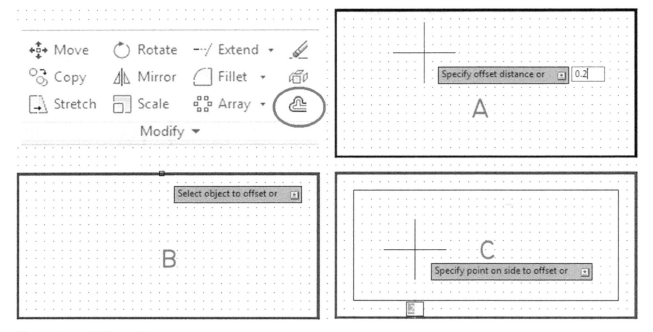

Fig. 4.3 – Offset Command

8. On Home tab → Modify panel → click on Offset tool.
9. You are prompted to Specify offset distance. Type 0.2 ↵ (Fig. 4.3 A).
10. You are prompted to Specify object to offset. Select rectangle. (Fig. 4.3 B).
11. You are prompted to Specify point on side to offset. Click somewhere inside the rectangle (Fig. 4.3 C). Another rectangle is created inside at a distance of 0.2.

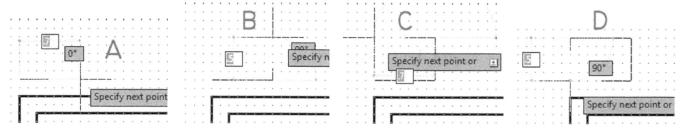

Fig. 4.4 – Line on Grid

12. On Home tab → Draw panel → click on Line tool OR Type L↵ .
13. Specify first point at 2 dots (0.2 units) above upper-left corner of outer rectangle (Fig. 4.4 A).
14. Move cursor to right. When you see 0.7, click to specify next point (Fig. 4.4 A). OR move cursor to right → Type 0.7↵ .
15. Move cursor up → click on 0.5 or Type 0.5↵ (Fig. 4.4 B).
16. Move cursor left → click on 0.7 or Type 0.7↵ (Fig. 4.4 C).
17. Click on first point (Fig. 4.4 D). Press Enter or ESC to finish Line command.
18. Similarly make a line inside this small rectangle as shown in Fig. 4.5 A.

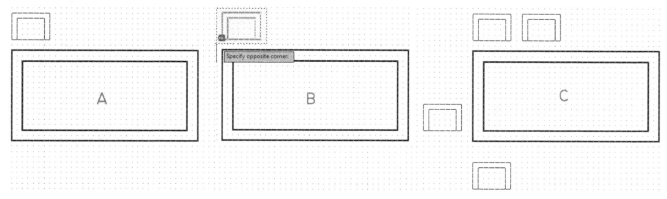

Fig. 4.5 – Copy Command

19. On Home tab → Modify panel → click on Copy tool. Prompt for Select objects appears. Select the small rectangle as shown in Fig. 4.5 B. Press Enter↵ to finish the prompt.
20. You are prompted to Specify base point. Click somewhere at a corner of small rectangle.
21. Click on other points shown in Fig. 4.5 C to copy objects. Press **Enter** or **ESC** to finish the Copy command.

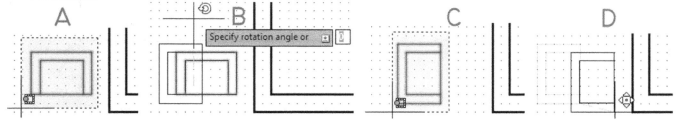

Fig. 4.6 – Rotate and Move Commands

22. On Home tab → Modify panel → click on Rotate tool. Prompt for Select objects appears. Select the small rectangle as shown in Fig. 4.6 A. Press Enter↵ to finish the prompt.
23. You are prompted to Specify base point. Click somewhere inside the small rectangle.
24. Move cursor to rotate the objects by 90° or Type 90↵ (Fig. 4.6 B). Press **Enter** or **ESC** to finish the Rotate command.
25. On Home tab → Modify panel → click on Move tool. Prompt for Select objects appears. Select the small rectangle as shown in Fig. 4.6 C. Press Enter↵ to finish the prompt.
26. You are prompted to Specify base point. Click somewhere at a corner of small rectangle.
27. Click 2 dots left of lower-left corner of big rectangle (Fig. 4.6 D). Press **Enter** or **ESC** to finish the Move command.
28. Similarly rotate the small rectangle on lower side by 180° and move it. Copy it to left (Fig. 4.7 A).

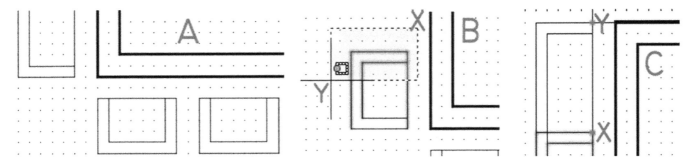

Fig. 4.7 – Stretch Command

29. On Home tab → Modify panel → click on Stretch tool. Prompt for Select objects appears. Select upper part of the small rectangle as shown in Fig. 4.7 B (Make crossing window (green – dashed outline) by clicking on X on right then Y on left). Press Enter ↵ to finish the prompt.
30. You are prompted to Specify base point. Click on top-right corner of small rectangle (point X in Fig. 4.7 C).
31. Move cursor to point Y in Fig. 4.7 C. Press **Enter** or **ESC** to finish the Stretch command.

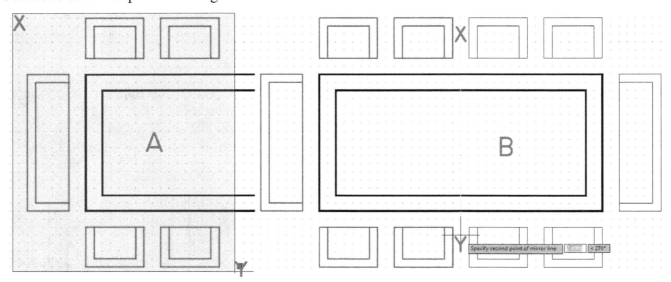

Fig. 4.8 – Mirror Command

32. On Home tab → Modify panel → click on Mirror tool. Prompt for Select objects appears. Select left part of the drawing as shown in Fig. 4.8 A. Make selection window (blue – solid outline) by clicking on X on upper-left then Y on lower-right. Objects completely inside the window will be selected and those partly inside will not be selected. Press Enter ↵ to finish the prompt.
33. You are prompted to Specify First point of mirror line. Click on point X (1 dot to left of selection up) as shown in Fig. 4.8 B.
34. You are prompted to Specify Second point of mirror line. Click on point Y (1 dot to left of selection down) as shown in Fig. 4.8 B.
35. You are asked **Erase source objects? N**. Press Enter (If you type Y ↵ , source objects on left will be erased).
36. Press **Enter** or **ESC** or **right-click** to finish the Mirror command.
37. The drawing shown in Fig. 4.1 is complete. Press Ctrl S to Save your work.

4.2 Trim – Offset – Array

Look at Fig. 4.9. A rectangle is repeated in polar array 3 times at 30°. Lines are offset at a fixed distance. Objects are trimmed inside rectangle or circle. Lines and arc are extended using grips.

1. Open Start.dwg and Save As **Ex10**.
2. Format → Drawing Limits → Type **0 , 0**↵ **25 , 15**↵ → Type Z ↵ A↵ .
3. Turn Object Snap (OSNAP) ON.

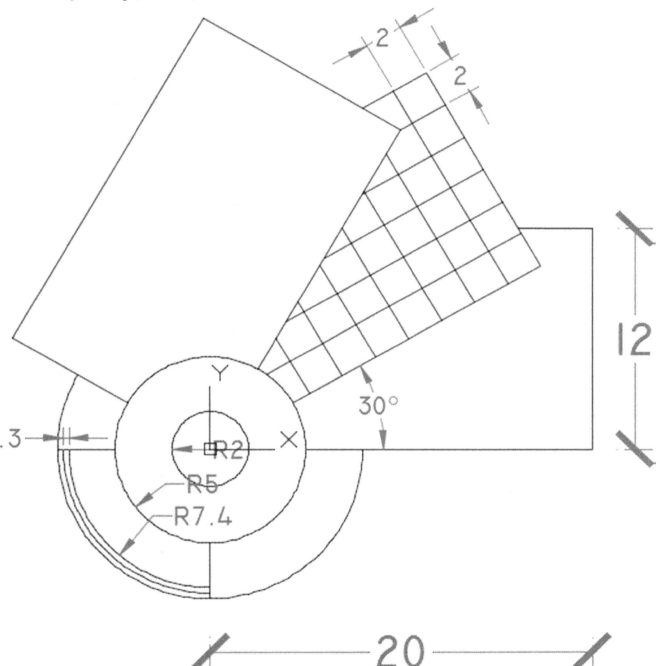

Fig. 4.9 – Trim – Offset – Array

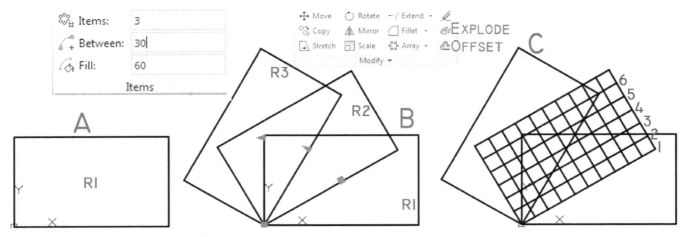

Fig. 4.10 – Explode and Offset Commands

4. On Home tab → Draw panel → click on Rectangle tool OR Type REC ↵ . Type **0 , 0** ↵ **20 , 12** ↵ . A rectangle R1 is drawn (Fig. 4.10 A).
5. Polar Array (Fig. 2.9) → Select Rectangle ↵ → Click on lower-left corner or Type **0 , 0** ↵ → Items = 3; Between = 30; Associative = Off → Close Array. You will get drawing (3 rectangles R1, R2, R3) as shown in Fig. 4.10 B.
6. On Home tab → Modify panel → click on Explode tool → Select rectangle R2 ↵ . The rectangle R2 explodes and each side becomes a separate line.
7. On Home tab → Modify panel → click on Offset tool → Specify offset distance = 2 ↵ .
8. Select line 1 and click anywhere towards line 2. Line 2 is drawn.
9. Select line 2 and click anywhere towards line 3. Line 3 is drawn.
10. Select line 3 and click anywhere towards line 4. Line 4 is drawn.
11. Select line 4 and click anywhere towards line 5. Line 5 is drawn.
12. Select line 5 and click anywhere towards line 6. Line 6 is drawn.
13. In the same way, offset lines on the other side (Fig. 4.10 C).
14. On Home tab → Modify panel → click on Trim tool → Select rectangle R3 ↵ . Click on each line inside R3. (if a line is not intersecting R3, it will not be trimmed. Delete it). Similarly trim R1 inside R2 (Fig. 4.11 A).

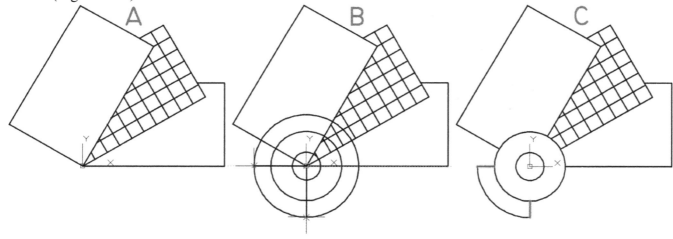

Fig. 4.11 – Trim Command

15. Draw circles of radius 2, 5 and 7.4 with center at (0, 0) (Fig. 4.11 B).
16. Line → Click at (0, 0) → Move cursor to left (see green tracking line) → Click on outer circle.

17. Line → Click at (0, 0) → Move cursor to down (see green tracking line) → Click on outer circle.
18. On Home tab → Modify panel → click on Trim tool → Select middle circle (radius 5) ↵ . Click on each line inside circle. (if a line is not intersecting circle, it will not be trimmed. Delete it). Similarly trim outer circle at two lines (Fig. 4.11 C).

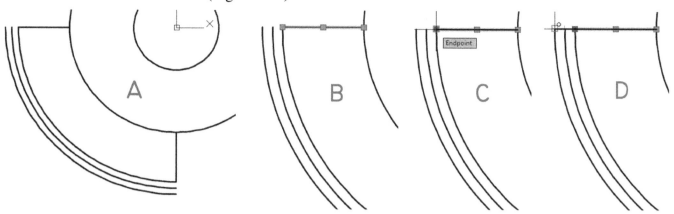

Fig. 4.12 – Offset and Grip

19. On Home tab → Modify panel → click on Offset tool → Specify offset distance = 0.3 ↵ → Select outer arc → click on outer side → Select outer arc → click on outer side (Fig. 4.12 A).
20. Click on line on left side → Three blue grips appear (Fig. 4.12 B) → Click on left grip. It becomes red (Fig. 4.12 C) → Move cursor to left side snap to end point of outer arc (Fig. 4.12 D) → Press ESC → Line extends to outer arc.
21. Similarly extend the line on down side.
22. Click on outer arc → Three blue grips appear (Fig. 4.13 A) → Click on lower grip. It becomes red (Fig. 4.13 B) → Move cursor to lower side of rectangle R1 and click (Fig. 4.13 B) → Similarly extend left grip to rectangle R3 (Fig. 4.13 C) → Press ESC → outer arc extends.

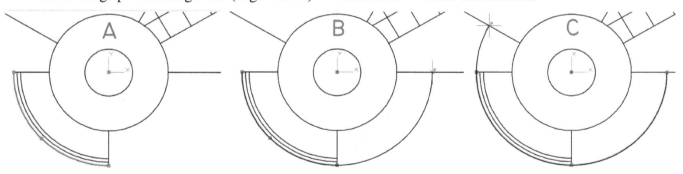

Fig. 4.13 – Extend with Grips

23. The drawing shown in Fig. 4.9 is complete. Press Ctrl S to Save your work.

Day 5 Organization and Information of Drawing

For better management and organization of a complicated drawing, you draw different objects on different layers. Information about spaces and objects is added in the form of text and dimensions. Hatches are patterns of lines used to give appearance of texture.

5.1 Layers – Text – Dimension

Look at the drawing in Fig. 5.1. It consists of a rectangle, hexagon and arc. Different styles and types of text and dimension lines are used in it.

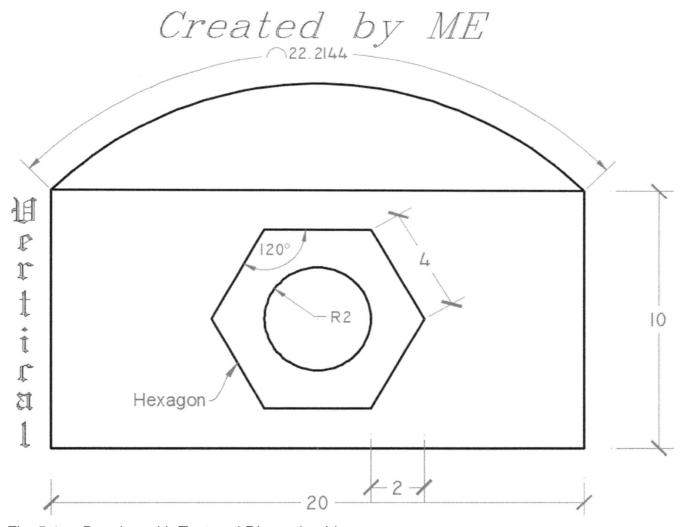

Fig. 5.1 – Drawing with Text and Dimension Lines

5.1.1 Draw Rectangle, Hexagon and Arc

1. Open Start.dwg and Save As **Ex11**.
2. Format → Drawing Limits → Type **0 , 0**↵ **25 , 15**↵ → Type Z ↵ A↵ .
3. Turn Object Snap (OSNAP) ON.
4. On Home tab → Draw panel → click on Rectangle tool OR Type REC↵ . Click somewhere in lower-left side of the drawing area. Type **20 , 10** ↵ . A rectangle is drawn.

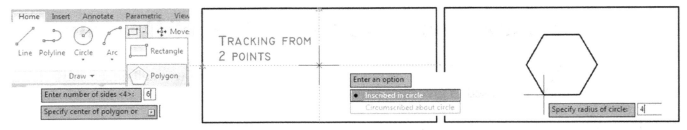

Fig. 5.2 – Draw Rectangle and Hexagon

5. Now you will draw a hexagon. Hexagon is a polygon with 6 sides. It will be inscribed in an imaginary circle of radius = 4.

    *   On Home tab → Draw panel → click on dropdown arrow on right of Rectangle tool. Click on Polygon tool.
    *   Enter number of sides → Type 6 ↵ .
    *   Specify center of polygon → Specify center of rectangle by tracking from 2 points as explained in steps 16 – 18 in § 2.3.
    *   Enter an option → click on Inscribed in circle OR Type I ↵ .
    *   Specify radius of circle → Type 4 ↵ . Hexagon is drawn.

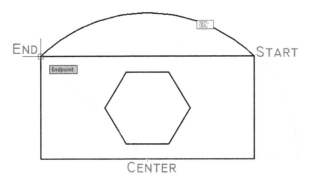

Fig. 5.3 – Draw Arc

6. On Home tab → Draw panel → click on dropdown arrow under Arc tool → Select the option Start, Center, End (Fig 1.16) → Click near the points shown in Fig 5.3. Arc is drawn.
7. On Home tab → Draw panel → click on Circle.
8. Specify center of circle with two-point tracking (Fig. 2.15 C – D, Fig. 5.4 A).
9. To Specify radius of circle, Type 2 ↵ (Fig. 5.4 B). Circle is drawn.
10. Your drawing will be as shown in Fig. 5.4 C.

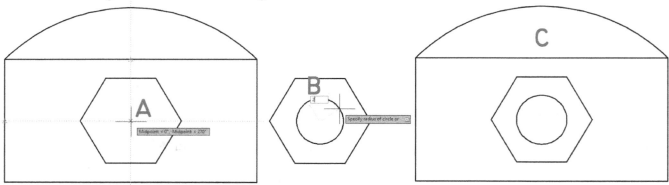

Fig. 5.4 – Draw Circle

5.1.2 Add Layers

Now you will add new layers and set their properties. (Layer 0 is always present).

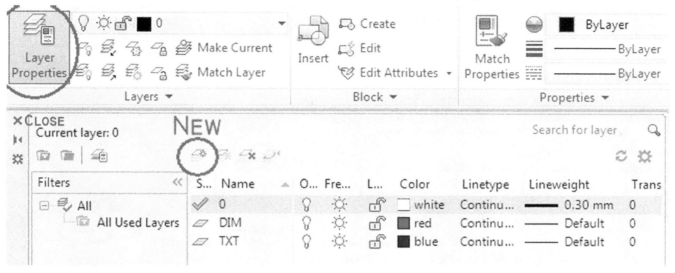

Fig. 5.5 – Layers

1. On Home tab → Layers panel → click on Layer Properties tool (Fig 5.5). Layer Properties Manager appears.
2. Click on New Layer icon 2 times. Rename layers, set color and lineweight as shown in Fig. 5.5.
3. Click on x (top-left corner of Layer Properties Manager) OR Layer Properties tool to close Layer Properties Manager.
4. Type LWD ↵ ON↵ . Drawing objects in Layer 0 are shown thick.

5.1.3 Text Styles

Now you will add new text styles and set their properties.

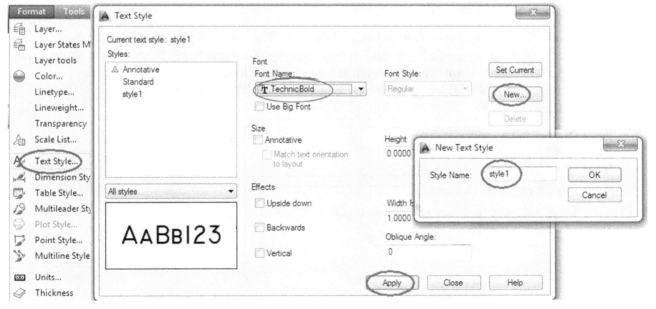

Fig. 5.6 – Text Style

1. On Format menu → click on Text Style… (Fig 5.6). Text Style dialog box appears.

2. Press New. New Text Style dialog box appears. Change Style Name as you like and press OK.
3. Select Font Name = Technic Bold. Press **Apply**.
4. New → Style 2 → Font Name = gothice.shx → Under Effects ☑ Vertical → Press **Apply.**
5. New → Style 3 → Font Name = romanc.shx → Oblique Angle = 20 → Press **Apply** → Press Close.

5.1.4 Dimension Styles

Now you will add new dimension styles and set their properties.

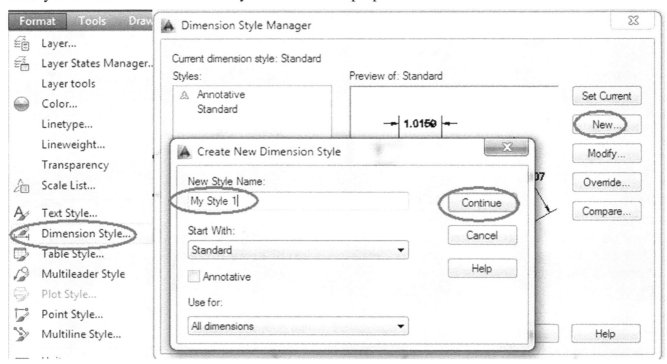

Fig. 5.7 – Dimension Style Manager

1. On Format menu → click on Dimension Style... (Fig 5.7). Dimension Style Manager appears.
2. Press New. Create New Dimension Style dialog box appears. Set New Style Name = My Style 1 as shown in Fig. 5.7 and press **Continue**. New Dimension Style : Style 1 dialog box appears.
3. On Symbols and Arrows tab, select Arrowheads = Architectural Tick (Fig 5.8).
4. On Text tab, select (Fig 5.8)
   - Text Style = style 1
   - Text Placement: Vertical = Centered
   - Text Placement: Horizontal = Centered
   - Text alignment = ⊙ Horizontal
5. On Primary Units tab, check 4 Zero suppressions check boxes (Fig 5.8).
6. Press OK.

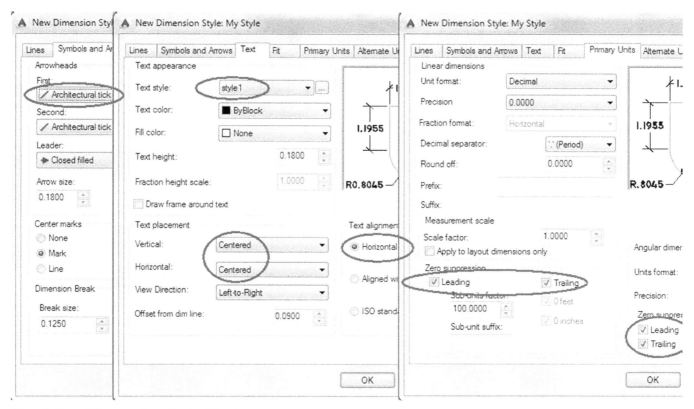

Fig. 5.8 – Dimension Style Settings

7. Repeat steps 7 – 11 above with New Style Name = My Style 2 (Fig. 5.9) and Arrowheads = Closed filled.

Fig. 5.9 – New Dimension Style

5.1.5 Linear Dimension Line

Linear dimension line is horizontal or vertical dimension line.

1. On Home tab → Annotation panel → click on Annotation dropdown → select dimension style = My Style 1 (Fig. 5.10 A).

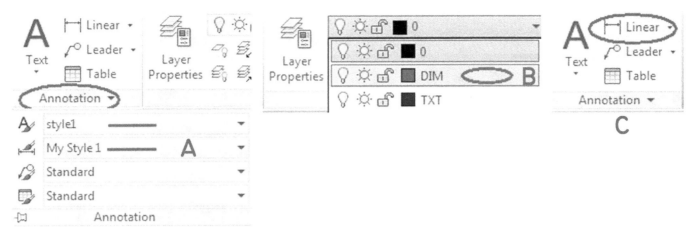

Fig. 5.10 – Select Dimension Style and Layer

2. On Home tab → Layers panel → click on Layer dropdown → select layer = DIM (Fig. 5.10 B).
3. On Home tab → Annotation panel → select dimension type = Linear (Fig. 5.10 C).

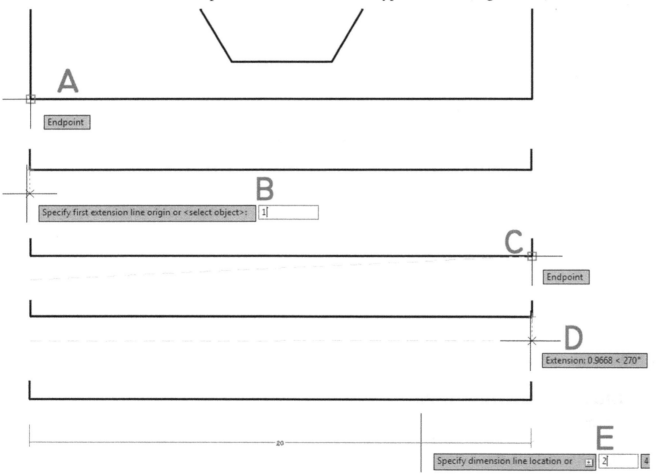

Fig. 5.11 – Linear Dimension

4. Bring cursor on lower-left corner of rectangle. You will see green square of Endpoint snap. DO NOT CLICK (Fig. 5.11 A).
5. Move cursor down along green dotted tracking line. Type 1 ↵ (Fig. 5.11 B).

6. Bring cursor on lower-right corner of rectangle. You will see green square of Endpoint snap. DO NOT CLICK (Fig. 5.11 C).
7. Move cursor down and CLICK (Fig. 5.11 D).
8. Move cursor down along green dotted tracking line. Type 2 ↵ (Fig. 5.11 E).
9. Dimension line appears. But its size is small. You will use a scale factor.

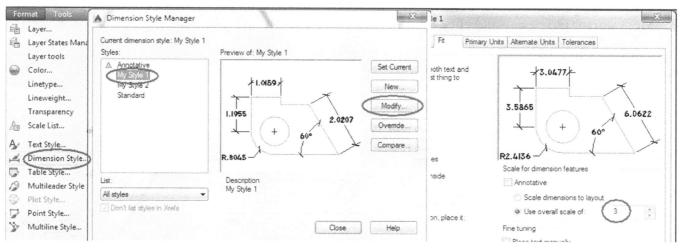

Fig. 5.12 – Scale Factor of Dimension

10. Format → Dimension Style → My Style 1 → Modify → Fit tab → ⊙ Use overall scale of = 3 → OK (Fig. 5.12).
11. Similarly for My Style 2 → Modify → Fit tab → ⊙ Use overall scale of = 2.5 → OK → Close.
12. Size of Dimension line increases (Fig. 5.13).
13. Repeat steps 3 – 9 to add dimension line on right side of rectangle between upper-right and lower-right corners (Fig. 5.13).
14. Repeat steps 3 – 9 to add dimension line below hexagon between lower-right and middle-right corners (Fig. 5.13).

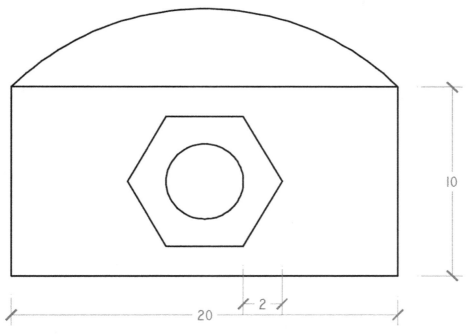

Fig. 5.13 – More Linear Dimensions

5.1.6 Aligned Dimension Line

Aligned dimension line is rotated dimension line.
1. On Home tab → Annotation panel → dimension type dropdown → select dimension type = Aligned (Fig. 5.14 A).
2. Click on upper-right corner of hexagon (Fig. 5.14 B) and then on middle-right corner (Fig. 5.14 C).
3. Move cursor little away and click to place aligned dimension line (Fig. 5.14 D).

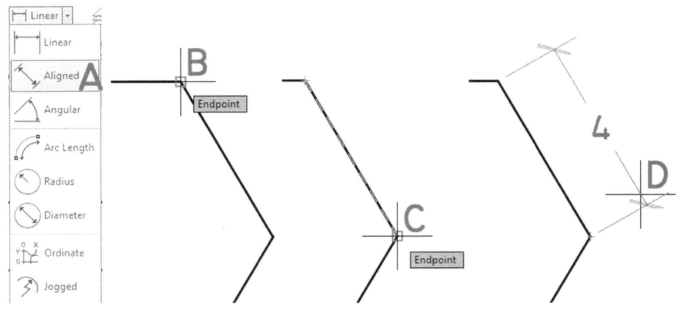

Fig. 5.14 – Aligned Dimension

5.1.7 Radius Dimension

Radius dimension shows radius of arc or circle with R symbol.
1. On Home tab → Annotation panel → click on Annotation dropdown → select dimension style = My Style 2 (Fig. 5.10 A).
2. On Home tab → Annotation panel → dimension type dropdown → select dimension type = Radius (Fig. 5.14 A).
3. You are prompted to Specify arc or circle → Select circle → Move cursor away and click to Specify radius dimension location (Fig. 5.15).

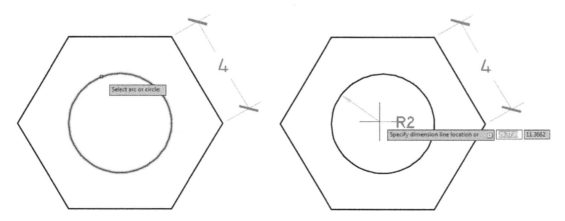

Fig. 5.15 – Radius Dimension

5.1.8 Arc Length Dimension

Arc Length dimension shows length of arc with arc symbol.

1. On Home tab → Annotation panel → dimension type dropdown → select dimension type = Arc Length (Fig. 5.14 A).
2. You are prompted to Specify arc → Select arc → Move cursor little up and click to Specify arc length dimension location (Fig. 5.16).

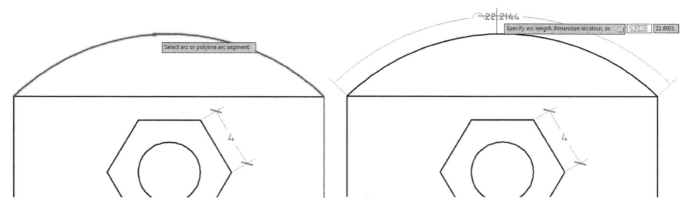

Fig. 5.16 – Arc Length Dimension

5.1.9 Angular Dimension

Angular dimension shows measure of angle with degree symbol.

3. On Home tab → Annotation panel → dimension type dropdown → select dimension type = Angular (Fig. 5.14 A).
4. You are prompted to Specify line → Select upper line of hexagon (Fig. 5.17 A).
5. You are prompted to Specify second line → Select upper-left line of hexagon (Fig. 5.17 B).
6. Move cursor little away and click to Specify angular dimension location (Fig. 5.17 C).

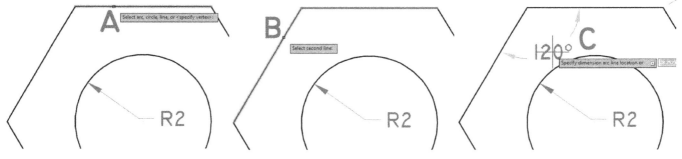

Fig. 5.17 – Angular Dimension

7. On Home tab → Modify panel → click on Explode tool (Fig. 4.10 B) → Select Angular dimension ↵ . The Angular dimension explodes and all parts (text, arcs, arrows) become separate objects.
8. Select text → A blue grip appears → click on the blue grip → it becomes red → drag it to bring text inside arcs (Fig. 5.18 A).
9. Click on arc towards upper side of hexagon → 3 blue grips appears → click on the lower blue grip → it becomes red → drag it to join with the other arc (Fig. 5.18 B).

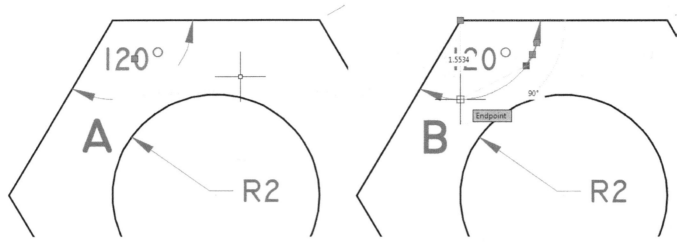

Fig. 5.18 – Angular Dimension Adjustment

5.1.10 Leader

Leader consists of text, line and arrow.
1. On Home tab → Annotation panel → select Leader tool.
2. Click on midpoint of lower-left side of hexagon (Fig. 5.19 A).
3. Move cursor down to specify leader landing location and click (Fig. 5.19 B).
4. Type Hexagon and click somewhere away (Fig. 5.19 C).

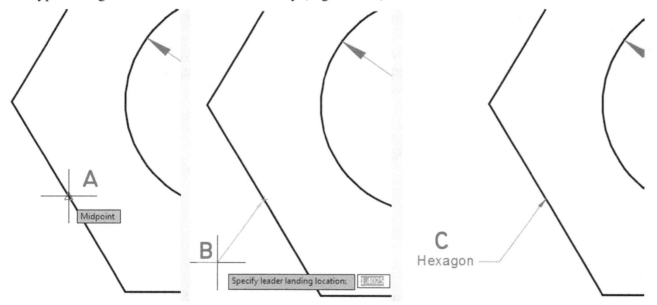

Fig. 5.19 – Add Leader

5. On View tab → Palettes panel → select Properties tool. Properties dialog box appears (Fig. 5.20 A).
6. Select the Leader (Fig. 5.20 B).
7. Adjust properties in properties dialog box as shown in Fig. 5.20 A.

- Under Leaders group, Leader Type = Spline
- Arrowhead Size = 0.6
- Under Text group, Height = 0.5

8. Properties of leader change (Fig. 5.20 C).
9. Press ESC. The Leader looks as shown in Fig. 5.20 D.

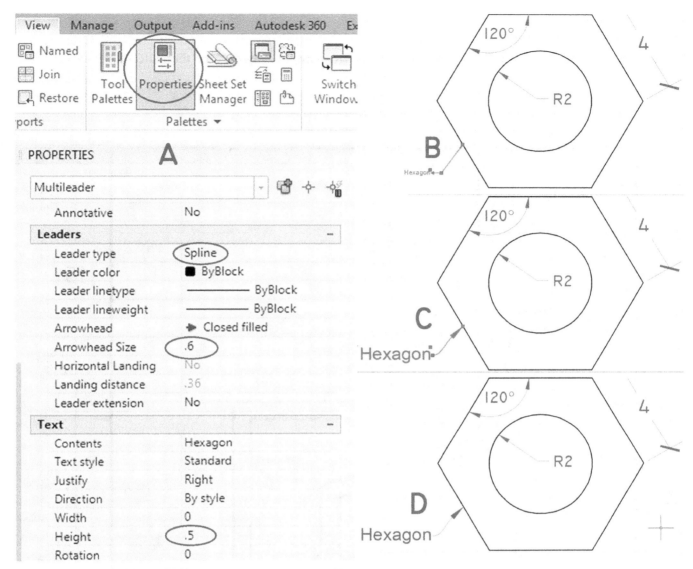

Fig. 5.20 – Adjust Leader

5.1.11 Add Text

To add text, you select or enter its style, height, angle and content.

1. From Layers dropdown, select layer TXT (Fig. 5.10 B).
2. On Home tab → Annotation panel → click on Annotation dropdown → select text style = Style 2 (Fig. 5.10 A).
3. On Home tab → Annotation panel → select Text tool.

    *   To Specify start point of text, click near upper-left corner of rectangle.
    *   To Specify height, type **1** ↵ .
    *   To Specify rotation angle, just press Enter.
    *   Type **Vertical** ↵ .
    *   Click somewhere else and press ESC.

4. Text in style 2 appears. Click on text. Click on blue grip. It becomes red. Drag to adjust its location (Fig. 5.1). Press ESC.
5. Repeat steps 1 – 3 to write text **Created by ME** in style 3.
6. The drawing shown in Fig. 5.1 is complete. Press Ctrl S to Save your work.

5.2 Hatch – Blocks

Look at the drawing in Fig. 5.21. You will start with this simple drawing and then add more features in it.

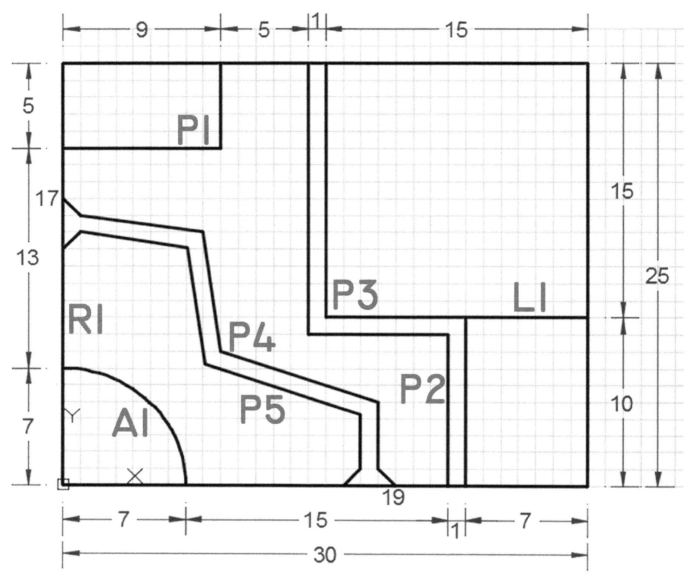

Fig. 5.21 – A Simple Drawing

5.2.1 Draw Rectangle, Polygon and Lines

1. Open Start.dwg and Save As **Ex12**.
2. Format → Drawing Limits → Type **0 , 0**↵ **40 , 30**↵ → Type Z ↵ A↵ .
3. Turn Object Snap (OSNAP) ON. Turn Object Snap Tracking (OTRACK) ON (Fig. 1.3 – 1.4).
4. Make grid settings as shown in Fig. 3.2 C.
5. Repeat steps in § 5.1.2 to add 4 layers DIM, TXT, PLANT and HATCH.
6. Repeat steps 1 – 3 in § 5.1.3 to add text style.
7. Repeat steps 7 – 11 in § 5.1.4 to add dimension style (Fig. 5.9) with Arrowheads = Closed filled and Scale factor = 7.
8. From Layers dropdown, select layer 0 (Fig. 5.10 B).

9. R1 : On Home tab → Draw panel → click on Rectangle tool OR Type REC↵ . Type **0 , 0**↵
   30 , 25↵ . Rectangle R1 is drawn (Fig. 5.21).
10. A1 : On Home tab → Draw panel → click on dropdown arrow under Arc tool. Select the option Center, Start, End.
11. For center, click on lower-left corner of rectangle (Fig. 5.22 point A).
12. Move cursor to right. Click when you see distance = 5 OR Type 5↵ (Fig. 5.22 point B).
13. Move cursor to left vertical side of rectangle and click somewhere (Fig. 5.22 point C).

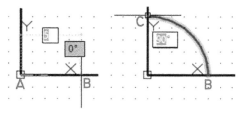

Fig. 5.22 – Draw Arc A1

14. P1 : On Home tab → Draw panel → click on Polyline tool OR Type PL↵ .
15. Bring cursor on upper-left corner of rectangle R1. You will see a green snapping square. DO NOT CLICK. (Fig. 5.23 A).
16. Move cursor down along tracking line. Click when you see Extension: 5 < 270 (Fig. 5.23 B).
    OR Type 5↵
17. Move cursor to right. Click when you see distance = 9 OR Type 9↵ (Fig. 5.23 C).
18. Move cursor up. Click when you see distance = 5 OR Type 5↵ (Fig. 5.23 D). Press ESC.

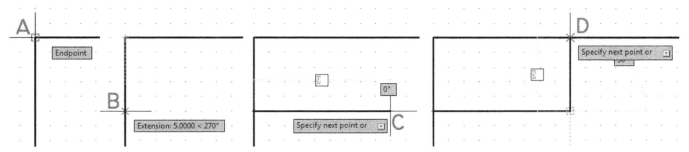

Fig. 5.23 – Draw Polyline P1

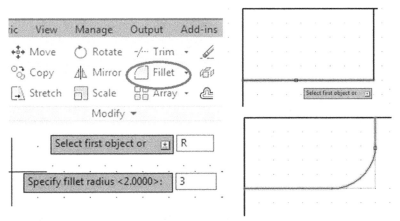

Fig. 5.24 – Draw Polyline P1

19. Now you will change sharp corners of P1into arc of radius = 3. On Home tab → Modify panel → click on Fillet tool OR Type F↵ (Fig. 5.24).
20. Type R↵ . Type 3↵ . Click on one side of P1 and then on other. Sharp corner change into arc.

21. P2 : On Home tab → Draw panel → click on Polyline tool OR Type PL↵ .
22. Bring cursor on upper-left corner of rectangle R1. You will see a green snapping square. DO NOT CLICK.
23. Move cursor to right. Type 14↵ .
24. Move cursor down. Type 15↵ .
25. Move cursor to right. Type 8↵ .
26. Move cursor down. Type 10↵ . Press ESC.
27. P3 : Offset tool → To Specify offset distance, Type 1↵ → Select P2 → Move cursor to upper-right and click.
28. P4 : On Home tab → Draw panel → click on Polyline tool OR Type PL↵ .
29. Bring cursor on lower-left corner of rectangle R1. You will see a green snapping square. DO NOT CLICK. Move cursor to right. Type 19↵ . (Fig. 5.25)
30. Move cursor 1 left – 1 up and click OR Type -1, 1 ↵ .
31. Move cursor 4 up and click OR Type 0, 4↵ .
32. Move cursor 9 left – 3 up and click OR Type -9, 3 ↵ .
33. Move cursor 1 left – 7 up and click OR Type -1, 7 ↵ .
34. Move cursor 7 left – 1 up and click OR Type -7, 1 ↵ .
35. Move cursor 1 left – 1 up and click OR Type -1, 1 ↵ . Press ESC.

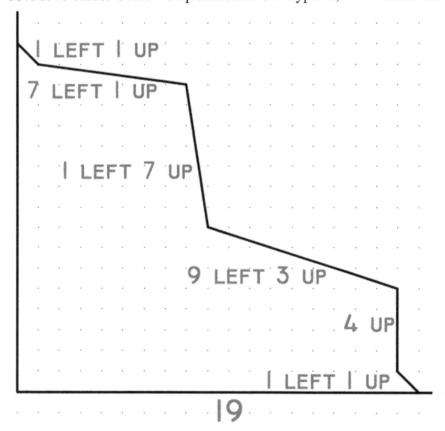

Fig. 5.25 – Draw Polyline P4

36. P5 : Offset tool → To Specify offset distance, Type 1↵ → Select P4 → Move cursor to lower-left and click. P5 appears as shown in Fig. 5.26 A.
37. Click on P5. Blue grips appear on each vertex. Click on lowest grip. It becomes red. Move cursor to place it to point (on grid) as shown in Fig 5.26 B.

38. Click on next grip. It becomes red. Move it to point (on grid) as shown in Fig 5.26 C. P5 appears as shown in Fig. 5.26 D. Similarly adjust vertices on the upper end of polyline P5.

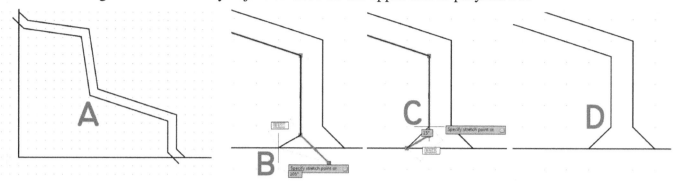

Fig. 5.26 – Draw Polyline P5

39. Draw line L1.
40. Now you will change sharp corners of P4 and P5 into arcs of radius = 2. On Home tab → Modify panel → click on Fillet tool OR Type F↵ (Fig. 5.27).
41. Type R↵ . Type 2↵ . Type P↵ . Select P4. Sharp corners change into arcs.
42. Repeat steps 40 – 41 for P5.

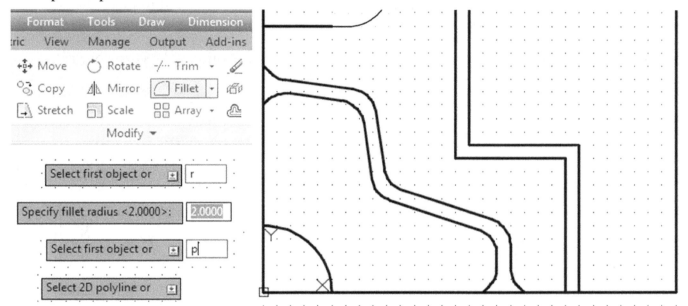

Fig. 5.27 – Fillet Polylines P4 – P5

43. Now you will trim rectangle at 4 points. On Home tab → Modify panel → click on Trim tool OR Type TR↵ . Make crossing window (green – dotted – First point on right – second point on left) to select objects as shown in Fig. 5.28. Press Enter.
44. Click on 6 points on rectangle shown with small red-cross.

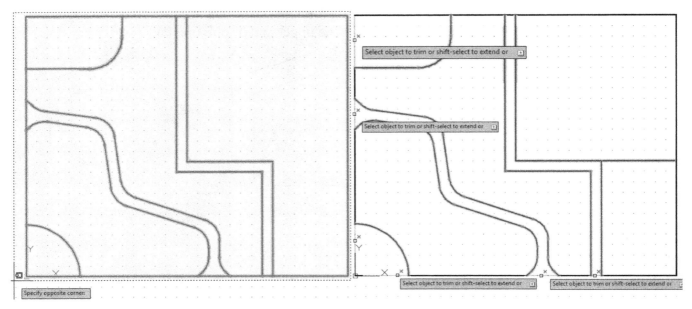

Fig. 5.28 – Trim Rectangle

45. Now you will mirror the objects. On Home tab → Modify panel → click on Mirror tool OR Type MI↵ . Select all objects (Fig. 5.29 A). Press Enter. To Specify first and second points of mirror line, click on points W and X (Fig. 5.29 B). Type Y↵ .

46. Type MI↵ . Select all objects (Fig. 5.29 B). Press Enter. To Specify first and second points of mirror line, click on points Y and Z (Fig. 5.29 C). Type Y↵ .

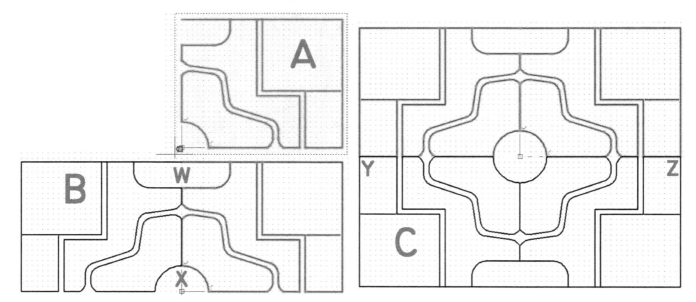

Fig. 5.29 – Mirror Objects

5.2.2 Add Text

To add text, you select or enter its style, height, angle and content.

1. From Layers dropdown, select layer TXT (Fig. 5.10 B).
2. Add text **Building** in upper-left rectangle as explained in § 5.1.11 (Fig. 5.30).
3. Copy this text in other places. Select each text and change its content and height in properties palette (View tab → Palettes panel → select Properties tool).

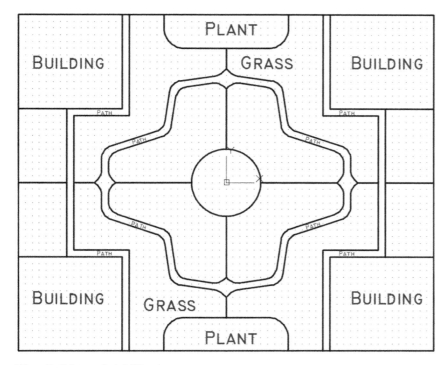

Fig. 5.30 – Add Text

5.2.3 Add Hatch

Hatch is filling a closed area with a pattern, solid color or color gradient.
1. From Layers dropdown, select layer HATCH (Fig. 5.10 B).
2. On Home tab → Draw panel → click on Hatch tool (Fig. 5.31).
3. On Hatch Creation contextual tab → Pattern panel → select Solid.
4. Click on colors dropdown → More Colors → Index Color tab → select Color 253 → OK.
5. Click inside PATH area.

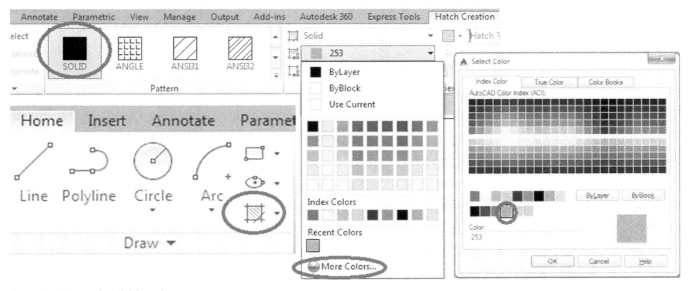

Fig. 5.31 – Add Hatch

6. Click on Hatch tool
   * Select pattern = Angle

- Select color = 34
- Set Scale Factor = 5 (Fig. 5.32)

7. Click inside 4 rectangles (2 on middle-left, 2 on middle-right).

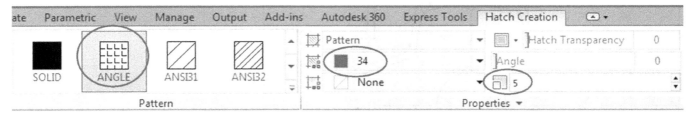

Fig. 5.32 – Hatch with Scale Factor

8. Click on Hatch tool
9. Click on Patterns dropdown arrow. All patterns appear.

- Select pattern = ANSI33
- Select color = 82
- Type Scale Factor = 7 (Fig. 5.33)

10. Click inside 4 Grass areas.
11. Drawing with text and hatching is as shown in Fig. 5.34.

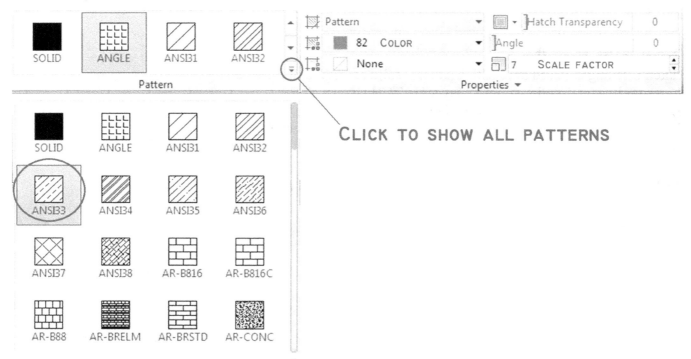

Fig. 5.33 – Hatch with Scale Factor

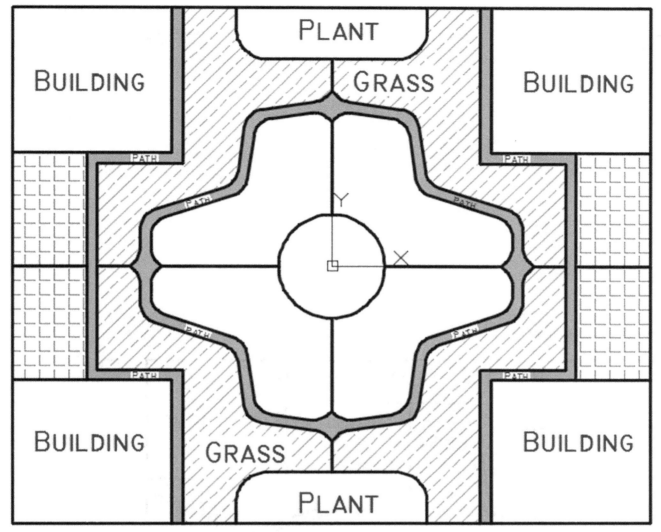

Fig. 5.34 – Drawing with Text and Hatching

5.2.4 Add Plants

Plants are CAD blocks. Blocks are separate drawings which can be inserted into another drawing. In this way, you can make and use reusable content.
1. From Layers dropdown, select layer PLANT (Fig. 5.10 B).
2. On Insert tab → Block panel → click on Insert tool (Fig. 5.35) OR from Insert menu, select Block…
3. Insert dialog box appears (Fig. 5.35).
4. Press Browse… and navigate to PLANT1.dwg in CADFiles folder.
5. Press OK.
6. Image of PLANT1.dwg appears. Move cursor to proper location and click to place the block.
7. In the same way, insert PLANT2.dwg and PLANT3.dwg.
8. Copy these blocks as shown in Fig. 5.36.

5.2.5 Add Dimension Lines

To add dimension lines, you select its style.
1. From Layers dropdown, select layer DIM (Fig. 5.10 B).
2. Add linear dimension lines as in § 5.1.5 (Fig. 5.36).

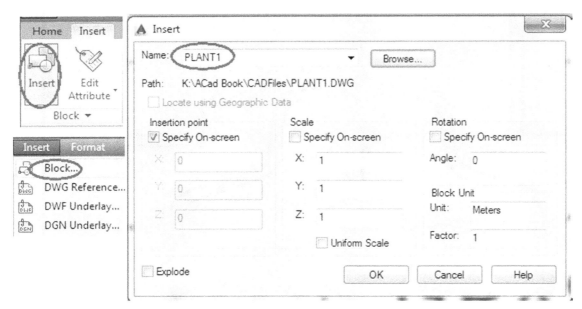

Fig. 5.35 – Add Blocks

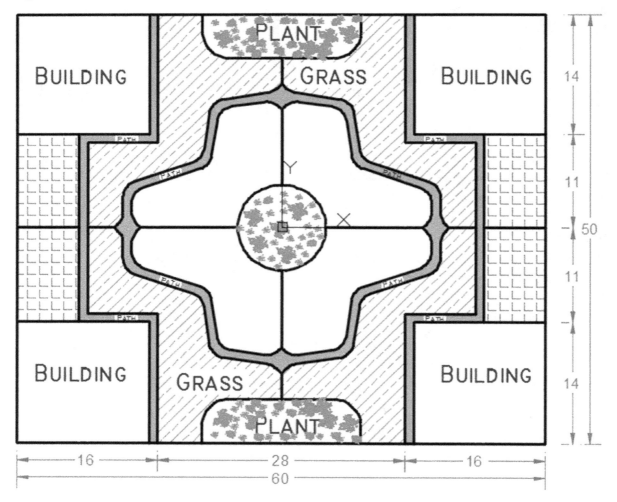

Fig. 5.36 – Complete Drawing with Text, Hatch, Blocks and Dimensions

Day 6   House Plan

In previous days, you have learnt enough skills that now you are able to make a house plan. The house plan looks roughly like Fig. 6.1. You will add furniture, fixtures and other details in it.

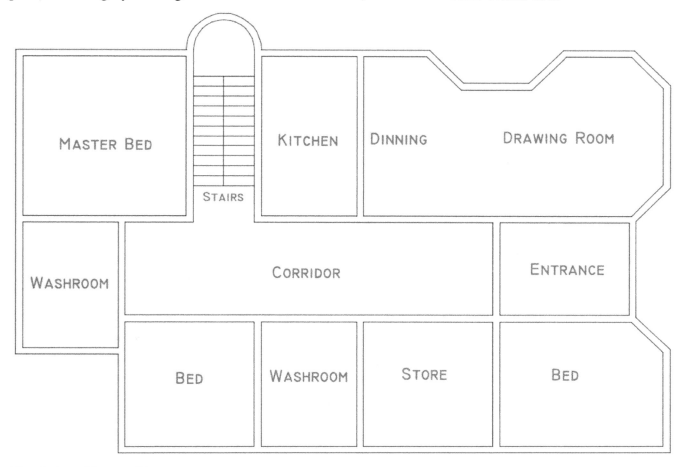

Fig. 6.1 – House Plan

6.1 Initial Settings

To start the plan, do the following steps.

1. Open Start.dwg and Save As **Ex13**.
2. Format → Drawing Limits → Type **0 , 0**↵ **30 , 20**↵ → Type Z ↵ A↵ .
3. Turn Object Snap (OSNAP) OFF. Turn Snap Grid (SNAP) ON (Fig. 1.3 – 1.4).
4. Make grid settings as shown in Fig. 3.2 C.
5. On Format menu, select Linetype… . Linetype Manager appears (Fig. 6.2).
6. Press Load… . From linetypes, select DASHDOTX2

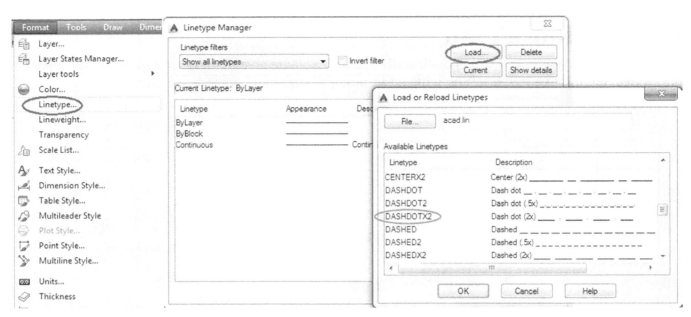

Fig. 6.2 – Loading Linetypes

7. Repeat step in § 5.1.2 to add layers as shown in Fig. 6.3.
8. Select Lineweight = 0.30mm for Layer 0 and Linetype = DASHDOTX2 for Layer Axes.

S..	Name	O..	Fre...	L...	Color	Linetype	Linewei...	Tran
	0				white	Continuous	0.30 ...	0
	AXES				red	DASHDOTX2	Defa...	0
	DIM				red	Continuous	Defa...	0
	DOOR-W				cyan	Continuous	Defa...	0
	FIX				32	Continuous	Defa...	0
	PL				green	Continuous	Defa...	0
	FUR				72	Continuous	Defa...	0
	HA				54	Continuous	Defa...	0
	TXT				210	Continuous	Defa...	0

Fig. 6.3 – Layers

9. Repeat steps 1 – 3 in § 5.1.3 to add text style.
10. Repeat steps 1 – 6 in § 5.1.4 to add dimension style (Fig. 5.8) with Scale factor = 7.

6.2 Draw Axes

Axes are vertical and horizontal dashdot lines. These lines will be drawn in layer Axes.

1. From Layers dropdown, select layer Axes (Fig. 5.10 B).
2. Draw a vertical line of length = 16.
3. On Home tab → Modify panel → click on Offset tool → Specify offset distance = 3 ↵ .
4. Select line 1. Move cursor to right and click anywhere. Line 2 is drawn.
5. Select line 2. Move cursor to right and type 4 ↵ . Line 3 is drawn.
6. Select line 3. Move cursor to right and type 3 ↵ . Line 4 is drawn.
7. Select line 4. Move cursor to right and type 4 ↵ . Line 5 is drawn.

8. Select line 5. Move cursor to right and type 5↵ . Line 6 is drawn.
9. Similarly draw horizontal axis lines (Fig. 6.4).

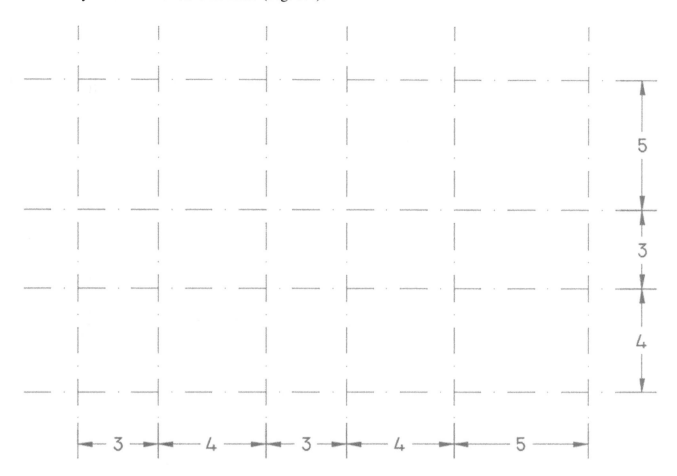

Fig. 6.4 – Draw Axes

6.3 Draw Multilines

Multiline is group of parallel lines. Number and type of elements depends on the style you choose. In this exercise, you will use the standard style which consists of two parallel solid lines. Make sure that you have selected User Preferences as shown in Fig. 1.10.

1. From Layers dropdown, select layer 0.
2. On Draw menu, select Multiline or ML↵ .
3. Type **J↵ Z↵ S↵ 0.2↵** .
4. Start by clicking on point A. Click on all corners as shown in Fig. 6.5 and finally click on B.
5. Right-click to end Multiline command.
6. Right-click again to start Multiline command again.
7. Start by clicking on point C. Click on all corners as shown in Fig. 6.5 and finally click on D.
8. Right-click to end Multiline command.

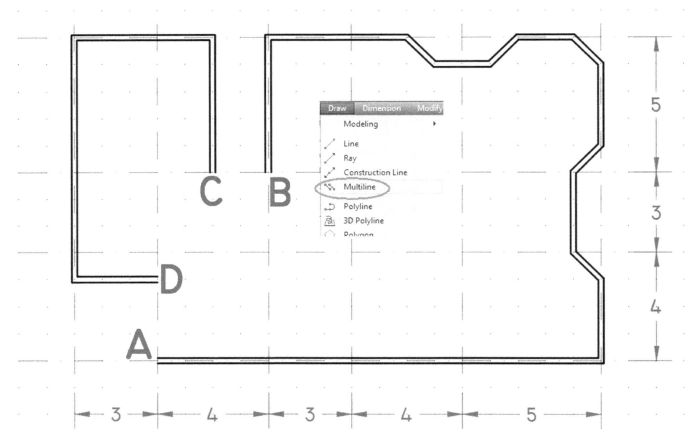

Fig. 6.5 – Draw Multiline

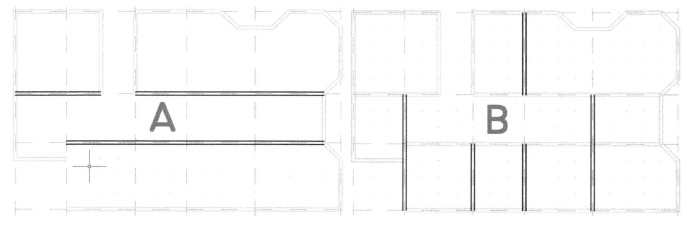

Fig. 6.6 – Draw Multiline

9. Right-click again to start Multiline command again.
10. Draw horizontal multilines as shown in Fig. 6.6 A.
11. Draw vertical multilines as shown in Fig. 6.6 B.

6.4 Edit Multilines

You will use some multiline editing options. Axis lines may be disturbing. You can hide them by turning layer Axes OFF.

1. From Layers dropdown, turn layer AXES OFF by clicking on the lamp symbol (Fig. 6.7). All objects on layer AXES become hidden.

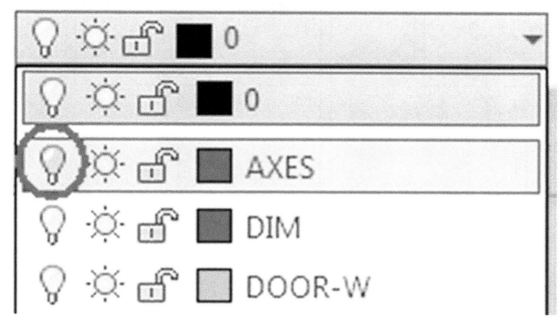

Fig. 6.7 – Turn Layer ON or OFF

2. On Modify menu → Object submenu, select Multiline… or type MLED ↵ . Multiline Edit Toolbox appears (Fig. 6.8).

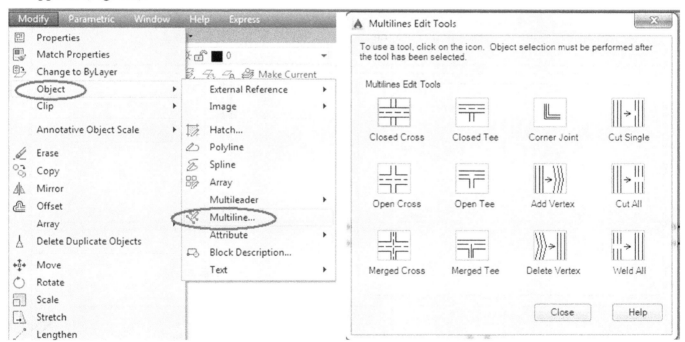

Fig. 6.8 – Multiline Edit Toolbox

3. From Multiline Edit Toolbox, click on Open Tee tool.
4. Click on X1 then Y1, X2 then Y2, X3 then Y3, X4 then Y4 (Fig. 6.9 A).
5. The multilines at tees are trimmed (Fig. 6.9 B).
6. Similarly trim all other tees.

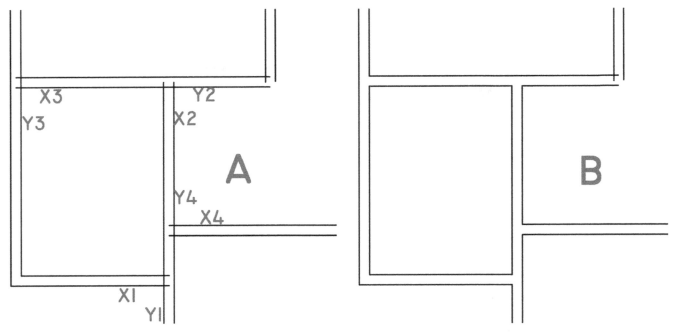

Fig. 6.9 – Multiline Trim Open Tee

7. Right-click to show Multiline Edit Toolbox. From Multiline Edit Toolbox, click on Corner Joint tool. Click on X1 then Y1 (Fig. 6.10).
8. Similarly trim all other Corner Joints.
9. From Multiline Edit Toolbox, click on Open Cross tool. Click on X2 then Y2 (Fig. 6.10).

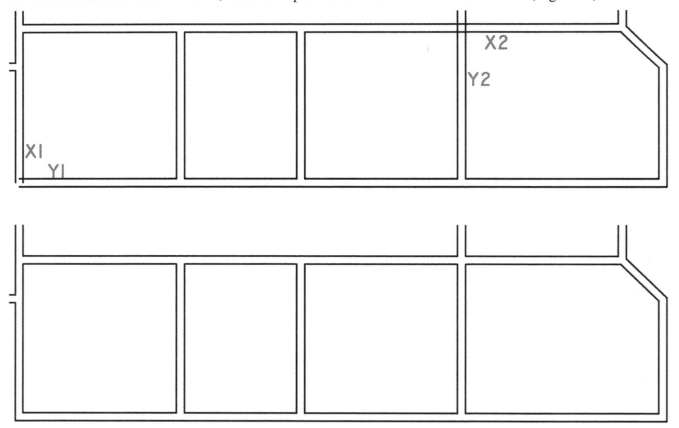

Fig. 6.10 – Multiline Trim Corner Joint and Open Cross

6.5 Stairs

Stairs are drawn as lines. You will draw one line and then make array.

1. Turn SNAP OFF and OSNAP ON (Fig.1.4).
2. On Home tab → Draw panel → click on dropdown arrow under Arc tool.
3. Select the option Start, End, Angle.
4. Click near the points S then E as shown in Fig 6.11 A. Make sure you see the green Snap symbols. Type 180↵ . Arc is drawn.
5. Repeat steps 8 – 11 in § 4.1 to offset arc at a distance of 0.2 (Fig 6.11 B).

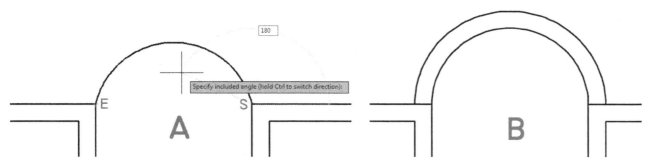

Fig. 6.11 – Draw Arc - Offset

6. Turn snap grid (SNAP) ON and object snap (OSNAP) OFF (Fig.1.4).
7. Draw line as shown in Fig. 6.12 A.
8. Trim ends of line (Click on Trim tool → select two multilines (Fig. 6.12 B)↵ click on ends of line).
9. Make array of line (Array tool → select line↵ Columns = 1, Rows = 12, Between rows = 0.3 (Fig. 6.12 C)).
10. Turn SNAP OFF and OSNAP ON (Fig.1.4).
11. Draw line from upper midpoint to lower midpoint (Fig. 6.12 D).

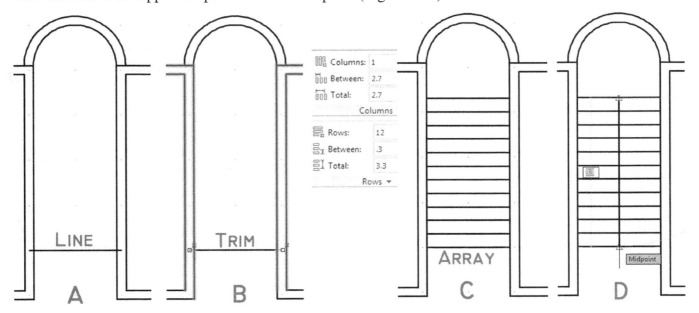

Fig. 6.12 – Draw Stairs

6.6 Fixtures

Fixtures are fixed objects such as sink, tub etc.

6.6.1 Fixtures in Washroom

You will place sink, toilet and tub in the washroom area near master bedroom.
1. Turn SNAP OFF and OSNAP OFF (Fig.1.4).
2. From Layers dropdown, select layer FIX.
3. Zoom to washroom area. (**Rotate wheel of mouse to zoom in or out. Press wheel and drag to pan**).
4. Repeat step 2 – 6 in § 5.2.4 to add SINK3.dwg. In the Block Insert dialog box (Fig. 6.13), write Angle = 270.

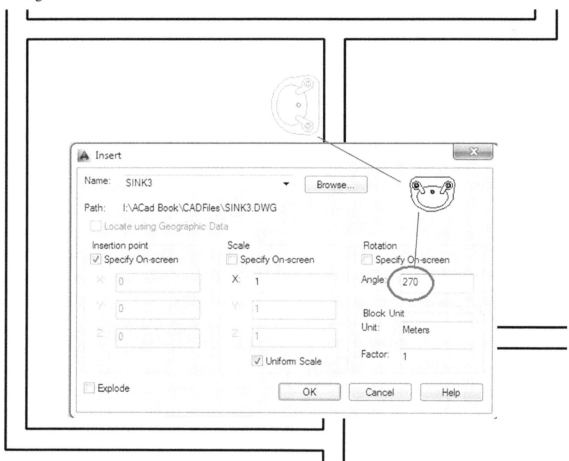

Fig. 6.13 – Add Block with Rotation Angle

5. In the same way, add TOILET1.dwg and TUB1.dwg with rotation angle = 180 (Fig. 6.14).
6. Similarly add fixtures in other washroom. (Mirror fixtures in left side washroom. Move to other washroom).

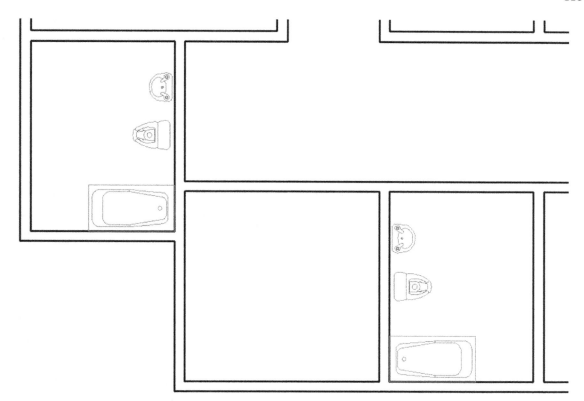

Fig. 6.14 – Washroom Fixtures

6.6.2 Fixtures in Kitchen

You will place kitchen sink and Oven in the kitchen area.

1. Zoom to upper side of kitchen area.
2. Add SINK2.dwg with rotation angle = 0. Move it so that its upper-left corner is on midpoint of upper line (Fig. 6.15). Mirror it.
3. Add OVEN1.dwg with rotation angle = 270.

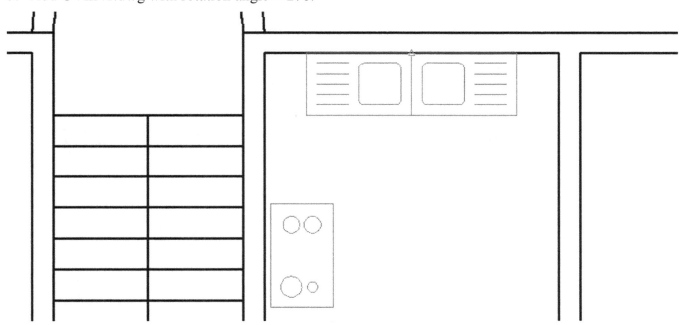

Fig. 6.15 – Kitchen Fixtures

6.7 Furniture

Furniture is movable objects such as bed, sofa, chair etc.

1. Zoom to Master Bed area.
2. From Layers dropdown, select layer FUR.
3. On Insert tab → Block panel → click on Insert tool (Fig. 5.34) OR from Insert menu, select Block...
4. Insert dialog box appears (Fig. 6.16).
5. Press Browse... and navigate to BED1.dwg in CADFiles folder.
6. Make X: scale factor = 2. Press OK.
7. Image of scaled BED1.dwg appears. Move cursor to proper location and click to place the block.

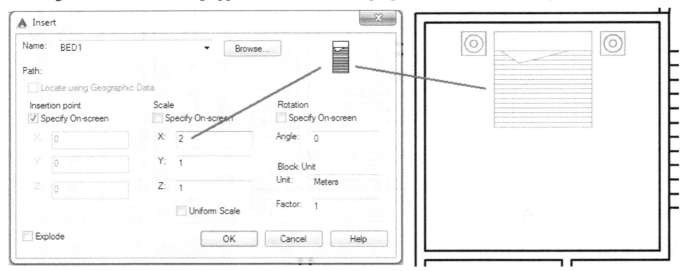

Fig. 6.16 – Block with scale-factor

8. Add TABLE3.dwg on one side of bed. Copy or mirror it to other side (Fig. 6.16).
9. In the same way add other furniture objects (Fig. 6.17).

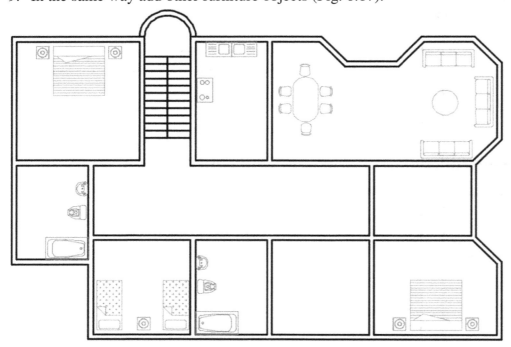

Fig. 6.17 – Furniture

6.8 Windows

Windows are added just like other blocks but snapped to grid for proper positioning.

1. Repeat step 6 – 8 in § 3.1 with Snap X Spacing = 0.5 and Snap Y Spacing = 0.5 (Fig. 3.2 C).
2. Turn SNAP ON and OSNAP OFF.
3. From Layers dropdown, select layer DOOR-W.
4. Insert → Block... → WINDOW1.dwg.
5. Place windows by snapping to grid. Insert one window. Use Copy and Rotate commands for others.
6. Some windows have X: scale factor = 2 (Fig. 6.18).

6.9 Doors

Doors are added just like other blocks but snapped to grid for proper positioning.

6.9.1 Add Doors

1. Repeat step 6 – 8 in § 3.1 with Snap X Spacing = 0.1 and Snap Y Spacing = 0.1 (Fig. 3.2 C).
2. Turn SNAP ON and OSNAP OFF.
3. From Layers dropdown, select layer DOOR-W.
4. Insert → Block... → DOOR1.dwg.
5. Place doors by snapping to grid. Add one door. Use Copy (C), Mirror (M) and Rotate (R) commands for others (Fig. 6.18).
6. For double-door, place one door and mirror it to other side.

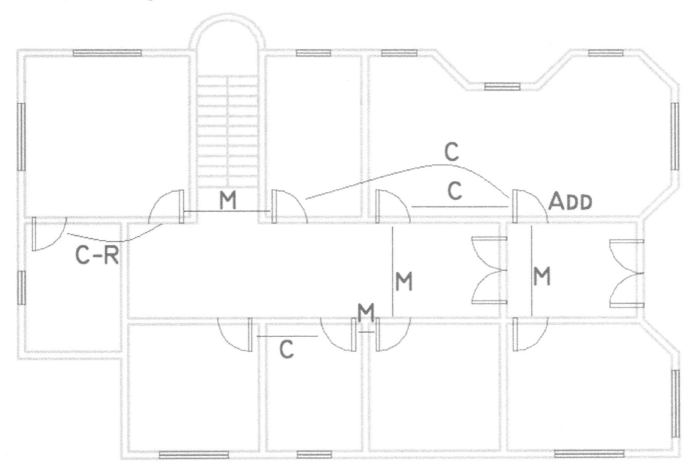

Fig. 6.18 – Windows and Doors

6.9.2 Remove Lines inside Doors

As you can see in Fig. 6.18, there are lines inside doors. These lines need to be removed. There are many ways. One easy way is to explode the multilines into ordinary lines and trim them.

1. On Home tab → Modify panel → click on Explode tool (Fig. 6.19).
2. Select all Multilines → Press Enter. The Multilines explode and become lines.

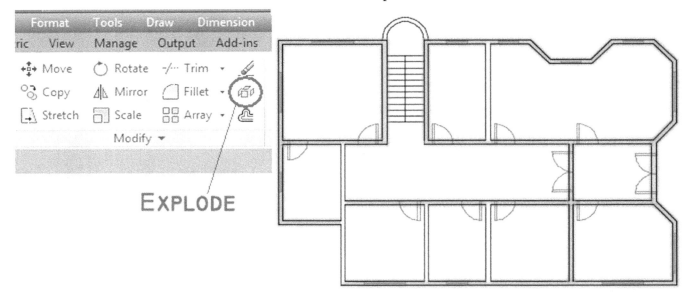

Fig. 6.19 – Explode Multilines

3. On Home tab → Modify panel → click on Trim tool.
4. Select the whole drawing → right-click.
5. Now click on the lines inside the doors. The lines will be removed (Fig. 6.20). Delete any remaining small line. (**Rotate wheel of mouse to zoom in or out. Press wheel and drag to pan**).

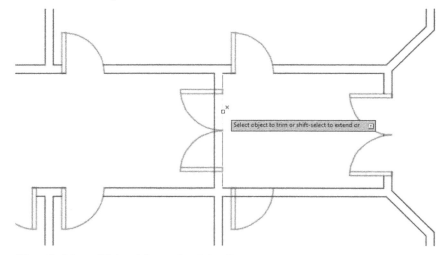

Fig. 6.20 – Trim Lines inside Doors

6.10 Text

To add text, you select or enter its style, height, angle and content.

1. From Layers dropdown, select layer TXT.
2. Add text **Bedroom** in a bedroom as explained in § 5.2.2 (Fig. 5.30). Set Text Height = 0.3.

3. Copy this text in other places. Double-click each text, change its content and click somewhere away.

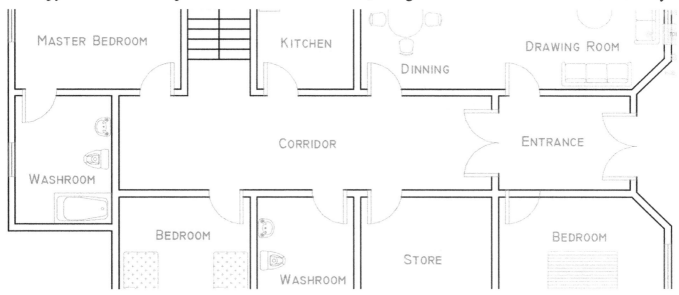

Fig. 6.21 – Add Text

6.11 Hatch and Dimension

You will add hatch patterns. First you will add lines or polylines in layer PL to enclose areas. Then you will add hatches. After that you will turn off layer PL.
1. From Layers dropdown, select layer PL.
2. Draw lines, rectangles or polylines (Green lines shown in Fig. 6.22).

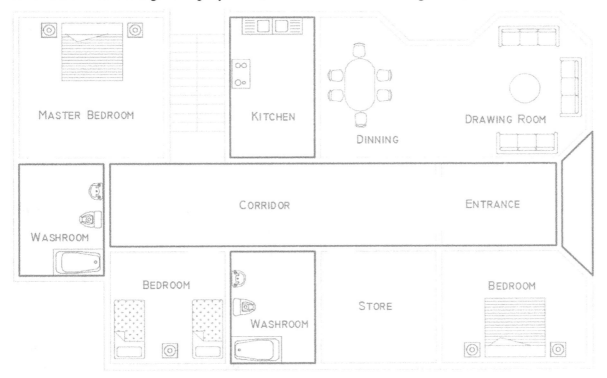

Fig. 6.22 – Draw Lines, Rectangles or Polylines

3. From Layers dropdown, select layer HA.
4. Turn off layer DOOR-W.
5. Add hatches as explained in § 5.2.3.
6. Turn on layer DOOR-W. Turn off layer PL. Turn on layer AXES.
7. Add dimensions as explained in § 5.1.5.
8. Complete House Plan looks like Fig. 6.23.

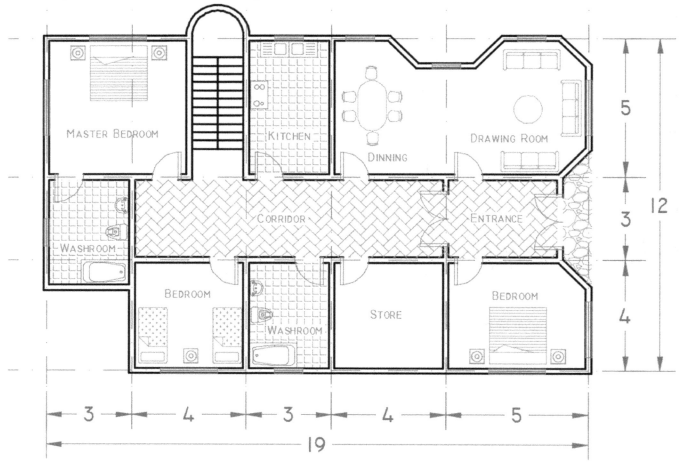

Fig. 6.23 – Complete House Plan

6.12 Simple Plot

After completing the drawing, you need to plot it. You can plot the drawing directly to a printer attached to your computer or plot it as a file and print it on paper later. Watch video in CADFiles folder in Download Folder (page v).

1. Type PLOT ↵ or Ctrl-P. Plot dialog box appears (Fig. 6.24).
2. Select

- Printer/Plotter Name = DWG to PDF.pc3 (or your printer)
- Paper Size = ISO A4 (297.00 x 210.00 MM)
- Plot Area = Window (Make a window from upper-left to lower-right side to select the whole drawing so that the drawing just fits in the window with little margins).
- Plot Scale = ☑ Fit to paper
- Check ☑ Center to plot

- Drawing Orientation = ⊙ Landscape (If you don't see this, click ➤ on right side of Help button).
- Select Plot style table = acad.ctb

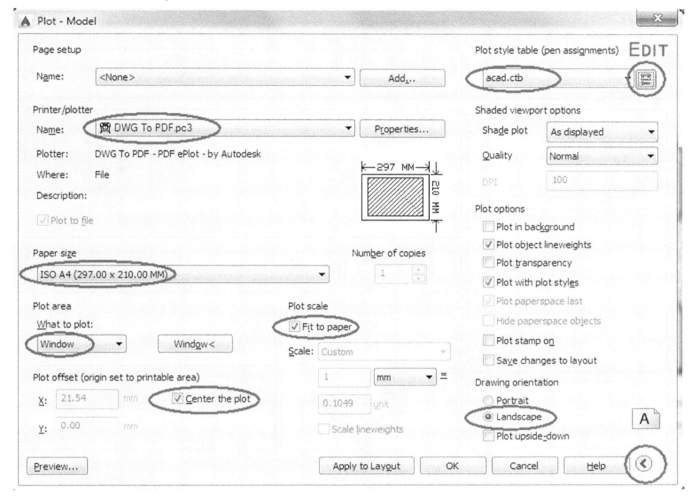

Fig. 6.24 – Plot Options

3. Lines in color 7 are drawn thick because lineweight for layer 0 is 0.3 mm.
4. Click on Edit button to the right side of Plot style table dropdown.
5. Click on Color 7. Select Line weight = 0.7000 mm.
6. Save As… My Plot.
7. Press Save & Close (Fig. 6.25).
8. Select Plot style table = My Plot
9. Press Preview… to see the plot.
10. Right-click on the plot. From floating menu, select Plot.
11. Save the .pdf file.
12. In this way, you can select any Plot style table e.g.

- Monochrome = all black
- Grayscale = all black with shades of gray

13. You can edit these Plot style tables to make pen assignments and save as another name. Later on you can use these Plot style tables in any other drawing.

Fig. 6.25 – Pen Edit

Day 7   Typical Floor Plan of a Multistory Building

In previous days, you used blocks as reusable objects. Sometimes you need to work on a drawing with repetitive set of drawing objects e.g. in a hotel, many wings have similar plan and in each wing, all rooms have similar geometry and settings. If you copy similar objects many times, there are two problems:

- The size of the drawing increases. Large drawings use a lot of computer resources and performance of the computer is affected.
- If you want to make alterations in one room, you will do it many times and a lot time is wasted.

In this situation, it is very efficient to use external references. Using external references to save time and computer resources is explained today.

You will draw a room as a Unit. This Unit is used to make a Wing. Many Wings are combined to make a Typical floor plan.

7.1 Draw Outline of Unit

First you will draw outline of Unit. Details of the Unit will be filled later on.

1. Make a new folder **MyHotel**.
2. Open Start.dwg and Save As **Unit** in folder MyHotel.
3. Format → Drawing Limits → Type **0 , 0**↵ **12 , 12**↵ → Type Z ↵ A↵ .

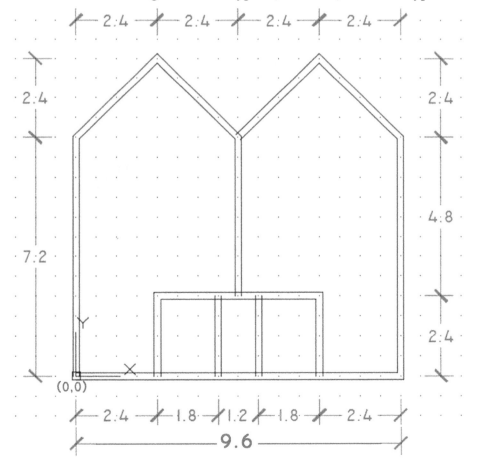

Fig. 7.1 – Unit Outline

4. Turn Object Snap (OSNAP) OFF. Turn Snap Grid (SNAP) ON (Fig. 1.3 – 1.4).
5. Make Snap and Grid settings (step 6 – 8 in § 3.1) with Snap X Spacing = 0.6 and Snap Y Spacing = 0.6 (Fig. 3.2 C).
6. On Draw menu, select Multiline or ML↵ (Fig. 6.5). Type **J↵ Z↵ S↵ 0.2↵** .
7. Draw Multilines as shown in Fig. 7.1. **Lower-right corner must be at (0, 0).**
8. Save file (Ctrl S) and Close (File menu → Close or click on x on upper-right corner. See Fig. 7.2).

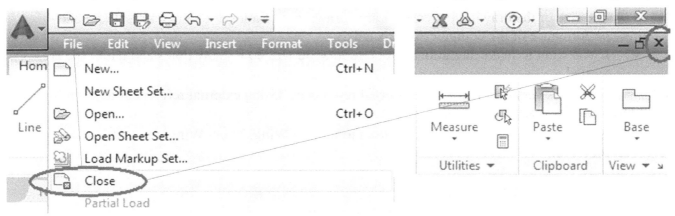

Fig. 7.2 – Close File

7.2 Draw Wing

Using the file Unit, you will draw one wing of the hotel.

1. Open Start.dwg and Save As **Wing** in folder MyHotel.
2. Format menu → Drawing Limits → Type **0 , 0↵ 30 , 20↵** → Type Z ↵ A↵ .
3. Turn Object Snap (OSNAP) OFF. Turn Snap Grid (SNAP) ON (Fig. 1.3 – 1.4).
4. Repeat steps 6 – 8 in § 3.1 with Snap X Spacing = 1.2 and Snap Y Spacing = 1.2 (Fig. 3.2 C).

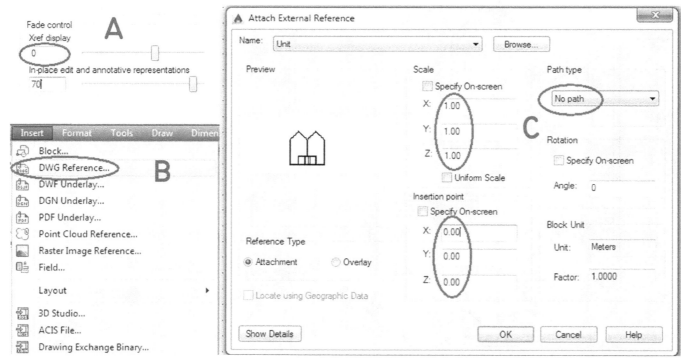

Fig. 7.3 – Attach External Reference

5. In AutoCAD Options (Fig. 1.8) → Display tab (Fig. 1.9) → Fade Control frame → Xref display = 0 (Fig. 7.3 A).
6. Insert menu → DWG Reference (Fig. 7.3 B). Attach External Reference dialog box appears.
7. Browse to saved file Unit. Make settings as shown in Fig. 7.3 C and press OK. Drawing of file Unit is attached.
8. Using Array command (steps 14 – 16 in § 2.1), make rectangular array of attached file Unit (Columns = 4, Between columns = 9.6, Rows = 1).
9. Using Mirror command, make mirror of the array of file Unit (Fig. 7.4). Mirror Line is 1.2 meters below.

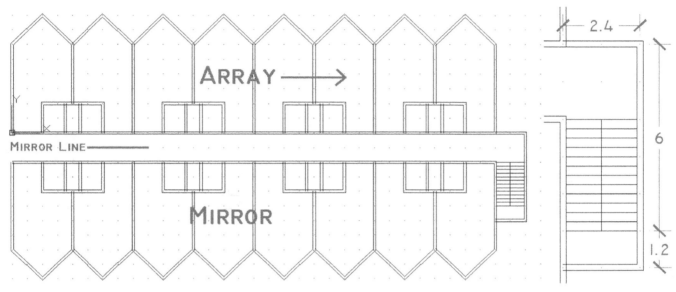

Fig. 7.4 – Array and Mirror

10. For stairs, draw multiline as shown in Fig. 7.4. Then repeat steps 6 – 11 in § 6.5. (In rectangular array of line, Columns = 1, Rows = 13, Between rows = – 0.3).
11. Save file (Ctrl S) and Close (File menu → Close or click on x on upper-right corner. See Fig. 7.2).

7.3 Draw Typical Floor Plan

Using the file Wing, you will draw typical floor plan of the hotel.

1. Open Start.dwg and Save As **Typical** in folder MyHotel.
2. Format menu → Drawing Limits → Type **0 , 0**↵ **30 , 20**↵ → Type Z ↵ A ↵ .
3. Turn Object Snap (OSNAP) OFF. Turn Snap Grid (SNAP) ON (Fig. 1.3 – 1.4).
4. Repeat steps 6 – 8 in § 3.1 with Snap X Spacing = 1.2 and Snap Y Spacing = 1.2 (Fig. 3.2 C).
5. In AutoCAD Options (Fig. 1.8) → Display tab (Fig. 1.9) → Fade Control frame → Xref display = 0 (Fig. 7.3 A).
6. Insert menu → DWG Reference (Fig. 7.3 B). Attach External Reference dialog box appears.
7. Browse to saved file Wing. Make settings as shown in Fig. 7.3 C and press OK. Drawing of file Wing is attached.
8. On Home tab → Modify panel → click on dropdown arrow to the right of Array tool and select Polar Array (Fig. 2.9). Prompt for Select objects appears. Click on drawing of Wing to select it. Press Enter ↵ to finish the prompt.
9. You are prompted to Specify center point of array. Type **– 14.4 , – 1.2** ↵ .
10. Array Creation contextual tab appears. Set Items = 3, Between = 90.
11. Click on Close Array to finish the Array command. A polar array appears (Fig. 7.5).

12. Add 3 multilines as shown in Fig. 7.6.
13. Add layers AXES and DIM. Draw axes (§ 6.2). Add Dimensions (§ 5.1.5).

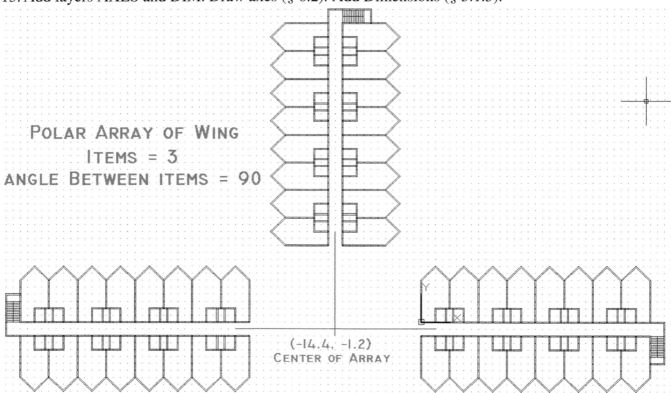

Fig. 7.5 – Polar Array of Wing

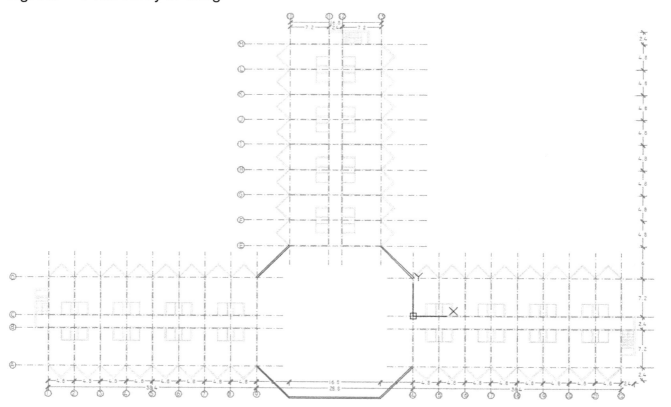

Fig. 7.6 – Multilines, Axes and Dimensions

14. Select layer DIM. Draw circles and write text inside circles to mark the axes. Draw one circle and write text in it. Copy it to other places. Double-click on each text and change it.

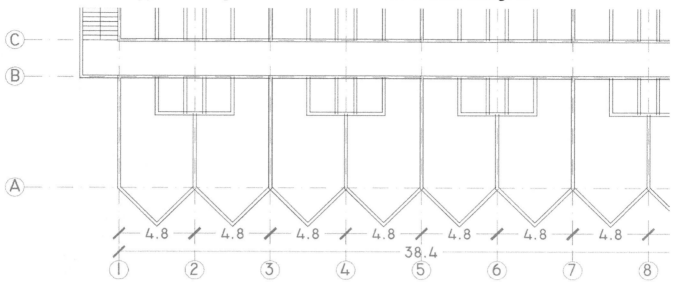

Fig. 7.7 – Circles and Text

15. Save file (Ctrl S) and Close (File menu → Close or click on x on upper-right corner. See Fig. 7.2).

7.4 Add Details to Outline of Unit

You will open file Unit and add details.

1. Open Unit.dwg in folder MyHotel.
2. Trim Corner Joints and Open Tees using techniques explained in § 6.4.
3. Add layers FIX, FUR, HA, DOOR-W as explained in § 5.1.2.
4. Add Fixtures in layer FIX as explained in § 6.6.1.
5. Add Furniture in layer FUR as explained in § 6.7.
6. Add Windows in layer DOOR-W as explained in § 6.8.
7. Add Doors in layer DOOR-W as explained in § 6.9.
8. Add Hatch in layer HA as explained in § 6.11.
9. Add objects as shown in Fig. 7.8.

    • Add all objects on left side.
    • Draw a vertical line in the middle in layer HA. This line will be used as mirror line.
    • Turn off layer 0.
    • Use Mirror command. Select all objects and mirror them to the other side.
    • Delete the line in the middle.
    • Turn on layer 0.

10. Save file (Ctrl S) and Close.

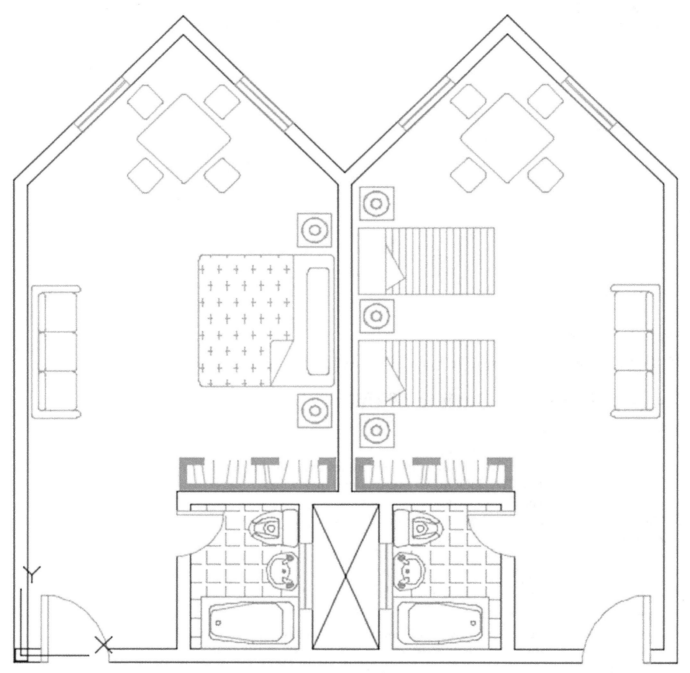

Fig. 7.8 – Details of Unit

11. Open Wing. You will see all details (Fig. 7.9). Close it.
12. Open Typical. You will see all details (Fig. 7.10). Your typical floor plan is ready.
13. If you make any change in Unit, it will be reflected in Wing and Typical.
14. If you make any change in Wing, it will be reflected in Typical.

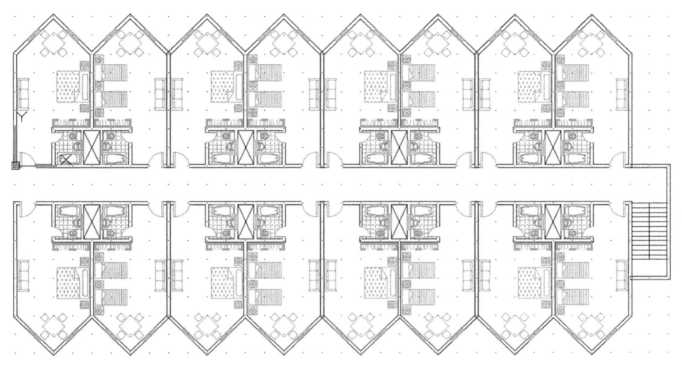

Fig. 7.9 – Wing with Details of Unit

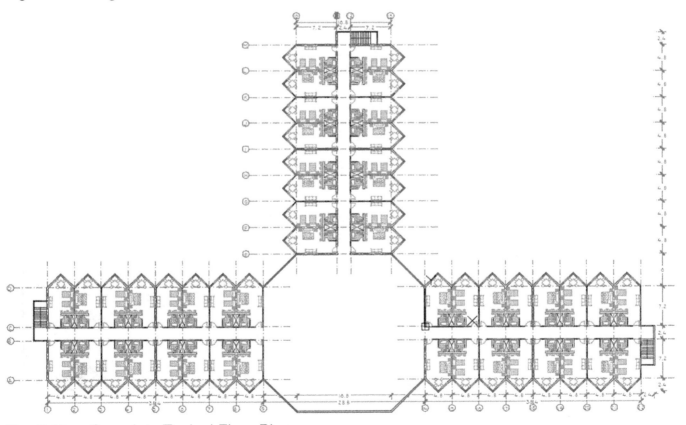

Fig. 7.10 – Complete Typical Floor Plan

7.5 Plotting on Titleblock

You will plot the typical floor plan on A1 title block with scale 1:200. Watch video in CADFiles folder in Download Folder (page v).

1. Open (double-click on) A1Block.dwg found in CADFiles folder in Download Folder (page v).
2. Make changes in the right side column. Change names of University, College, Department, Project, Done by etc.
3. Save As Typical_Plot in folder MyHotel.
4. You will see the title block. There are box symbols outside the four corners of the frame. These symbols show size of the paper.
5. Insert menu → DWG Reference. Attach External Reference dialog box appears.
6. Browse to saved file Typical in folder MyHotel.
7. Make settings as shown in Fig. 7.11 (Scale 1:200 = 0.005)
8. Press OK. Drawing of file Typical is attached. Move drawing in the middle of title block.

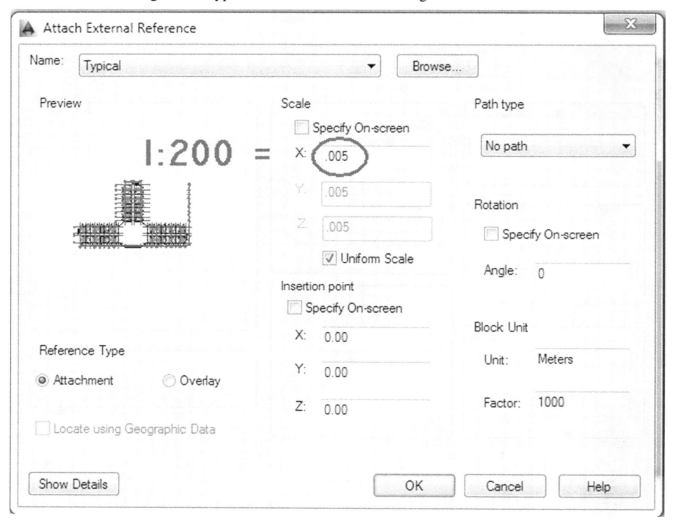

Fig. 7.11 – Attach Typical Floor Plan on A1 Title Block

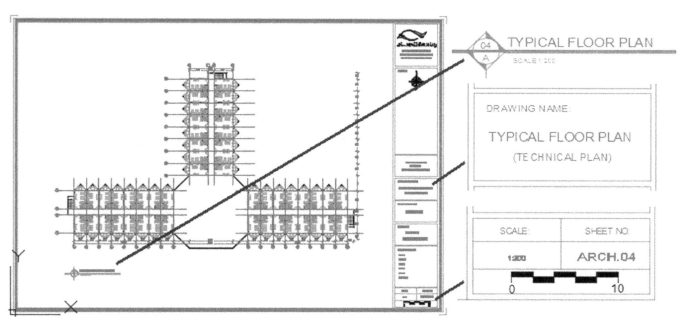

Fig. 7.12 – Typical Floor Plan on A1 Title Block

9. Insert block Sheet.dwg on lower-left part of the drawing. Explode the block and change text and scale (Fig. 7.12).
10. Add text for Drawing Name and Scale in right side column of the title block.
11. Insert block Scale.dwg on lower part of the right side column. Explode the block and change text (Fig. 7.12).
12. Type PLOT ↵ or Ctrl-P. Plot dialog box appears.
13. Select (Fig. 7.13)

- Printer/Plotter Name = DWG to PDF.pc3
- Paper Size = ISO full bleed A1 (841.00 x 594.00 MM)
- Plot Area = Window (Make a window snapping exactly to box symbols on upper-right corner then lower-left corner outside the frame).
- Plot Scale = 1:1
- Check ☑ Center to plot
- Drawing Orientation = ⊙ Landscape (If you don't see this, click ➤ on right side of Help button).
- Select Plot style table = acad.ctb

14. Press Preview… You will see the whole plot.
15. Right-click on the plot. From floating menu, select Plot.
16. Save the .pdf file.

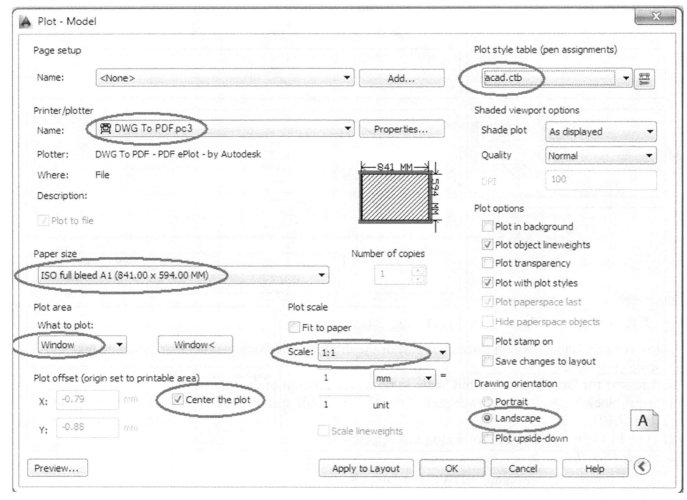

Fig. 7.13 – Plot Typical Floor Plan on A1 Title Block

7.6 Model Space – Paper Space

You will plot all three drawings (Unit, Wing, Typical) on A0 paper. If they are drawn normally in model space, they will have same scale and their size on the sheet may not be suitable. If you want to draw each drawing with a different scale, then you will place each drawing in a different viewport. You will insert them in model space. In paper space you will make a layout with three viewports. Watch video in CADFiles folder in Download Folder (page v).

1. Open (double-click on) A0Block.dwg found in CADFiles folder in Download Folder (page v).
2. Make changes in the right side column. Change names of University, College, Department, Project, Done by etc. because they are same for all sheets of the project. DO NOT ADD Drawing Name, Scale, Sheet No: because they are different for each sheet, so they will added on the sheet.
3. Save as MyA0Block.dwg
4. Open (double-click on) Plot.dwg found in CADFiles folder in Download Folder (page v). Save As A0_Plot in folder MyHotel.
5. Insert menu → DWG Reference (Fig. 7.3 B). Attach External Reference dialog box appears.
6. Browse to saved file Unit. Make settings as shown in Fig. 7.14 and press OK. Drawing of file Unit is attached.
7. Similarly insert Wing and Typical as shown in Fig. 7.15. All three drawings are in Model space (See Model tab at lower-left corner in Fig. 7.15).

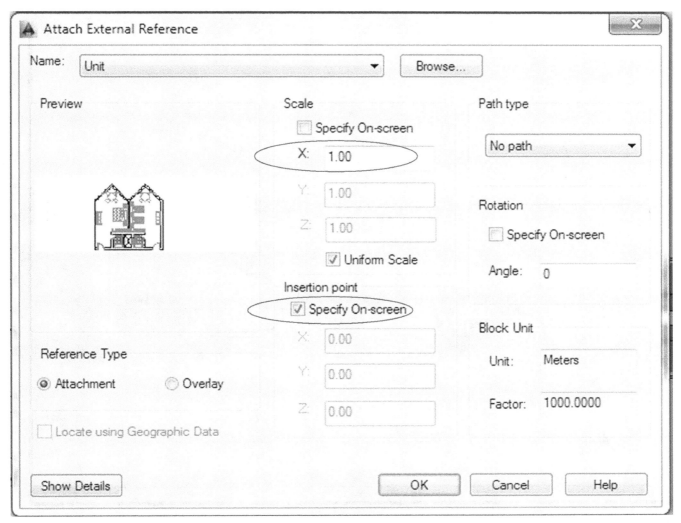

Fig. 7.14 – Settings on Attach External Reference Dialog Box

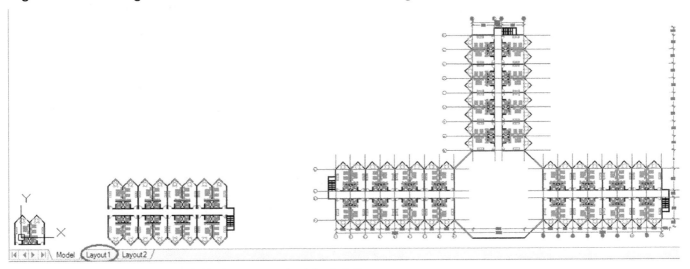

Fig. 7.15 – Insert External References in Model Space

8. Click on Layout1 tab near lower-left corner (Fig. 7.15).
9. You will see a layout with all three drawings in a viewport. Select the viewport with a single-click and press Delete (Fig. 7.16).

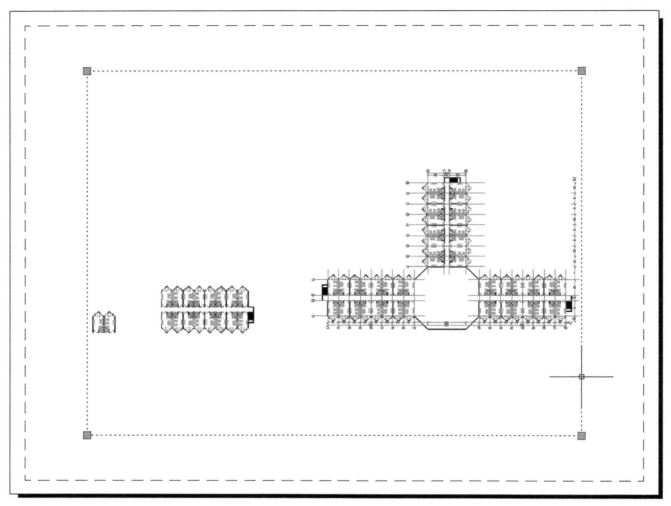

Fig. 7.16 – Layout with a Viewport

10. On Layout tab → Layout panel → click on Page Setup tool (Fig. 7.17 A) OR right-click Layout1 tab → click on Page Setup Manager… (Fig. 7.17 B).

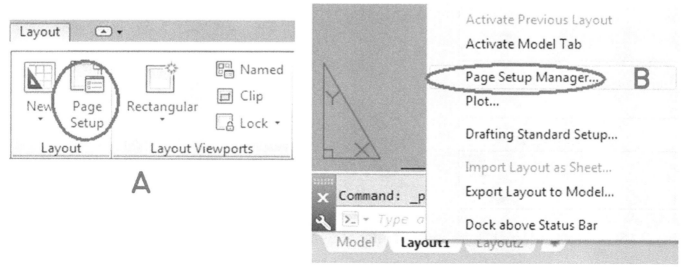

Fig. 7.17 – Page Setup Manager

11. Page Setup Manager Dialog box appears.

12. Click New… Name = A0Plot. Make settings as shown in Fig 7.18 (Similar to shown in Fig. 7.13 with Paper Size A0) → OK → OK → A0Plot – Set Current → Close.

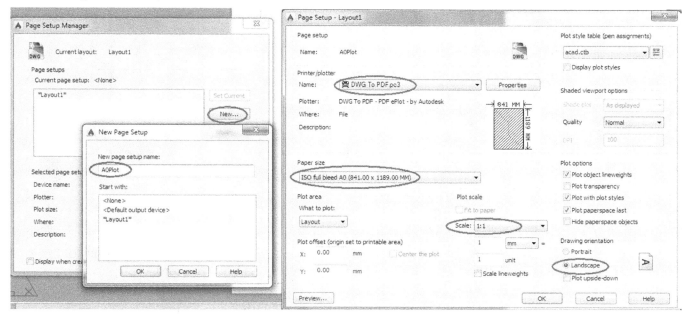

Fig. 7.18 – Page Setup Manager Dialog Box

13. Insert menu → Block. Insert dialog box appears. Browse to MyA0Block.dwg. Make settings as shown in Fig. 7.19. A0 title block fits in A0 layout (Fig. 7.20).
14. Select layer VPORT.
15. Draw three rectangles A, B, C and a circle D as shown in Fig. 7.20.

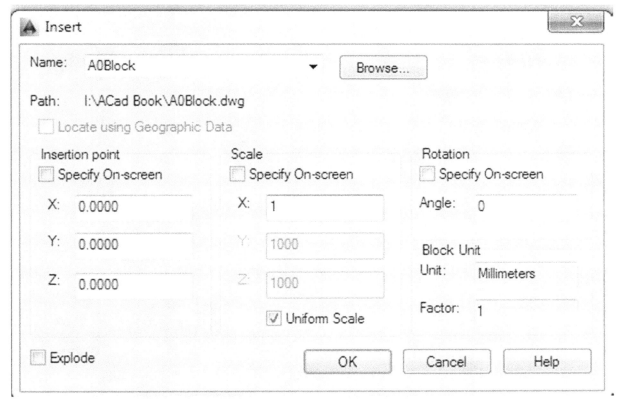

Fig. 7.19 – Insert A0 Title Block

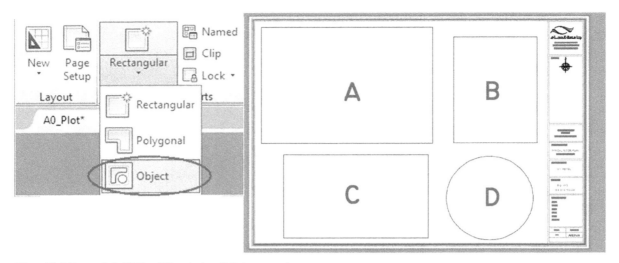

Fig. 7.20 – A0 Title Block in A0 Layout

16. On Layout tab → Layout Viewports panel → click on dropdown arrow under Rectangular tool → select Object tool (Fig. 7.20) → click on rectangle A → rectangle converts into Viewport (You will see the complete drawing inside it).
17. Similarly convert objects B, C and D into viewports (You can draw circle, polygon or closed polyline and convert it into viewport).
18. Double-click inside viewport B. Its border becomes thick. Rotate wheel of mouse to zoom in or out. Press wheel and drag to pan so that Unit drawing covers the viewport (Fig. 7.21).
19. On Status Bar, click on scale (Fig. 7.22). Select Scale = 1:50.
20. Double-click inside viewport C and zoom in to Wing. Set scale = 1:100.

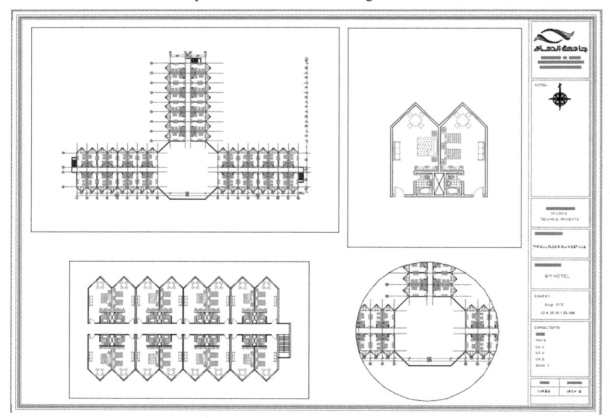

Fig. 7.21 – Zoom In to Views in Viewports

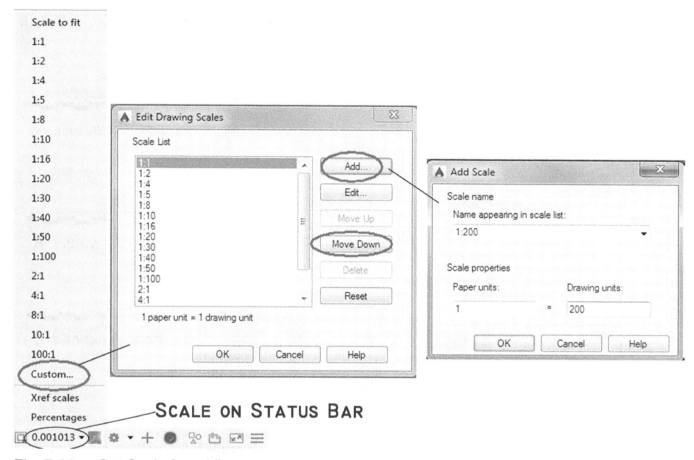

Scale to fit
1:1
1:2
1:4
1:5
1:8
1:10
1:16
1:20
1:30
1:40
1:50
1:100
2:1
4:1
8:1
10:1
100:1
Custom...
Xref scales
Percentages

SCALE ON STATUS BAR

Fig. 7.22 – Set Scale for a Viewport

21. Double-click inside viewport A and zoom in to Typical. The suitable scale is 1:200 but it is not present in the scale column. So you will add a custom scale.
22. Click on Custom in the scale column (Fig. 7.22). Edit Drawing Scales dialog box appears.
23. Click on Add…
24. In the Add Scale dialog box, type Name = 1:200, Paper units = 1, Drawing units = 200 → OK.
25. Scale 1:200 is added in the scale list. Press Move Down and bring it under 1:100 → OK.
26. From the scale column, select 1:200.
27. Double-click inside viewport D and zoom in to central part of Typical. Set scale = 1:200.
28. To rescale objects inside a viewport, double-click inside the viewport. The borders become thick. Now you can pan, zoom or rescale inside the viewport.
29. To resize the viewport itself, double-click outside the viewport, then make a gentle single click on the border of the viewport. Blue grips appear on the corners and middle of sides. To resize, make a gentle single click on the grip. It turns red. Now move it to resize the viewport. (You may need to turn Ortho ON).
30. To hide the viewport boundaries, turn off the layer VPORT.
31. Insert blocks Sheet.dwg and Scale.dwg under each viewport (Fig. 7.23),
32. Explode all blocks
33. Change the drawing name in the block Sheet:
34. For Viewport A, drawing name = TYPICAL FLOOR PLAN, Scale = 1:200
35. For Viewport B, drawing name = UNIT PLAN, Scale = 1:50
36. For Viewport A, drawing name = WING PLAN, Scale = 1:100

37. Change the last number in block Scale. (The number 5 is for scale 1:100. For scale 1:200, multiply it by 2. For scale 1:50, multiply it by 1/2).

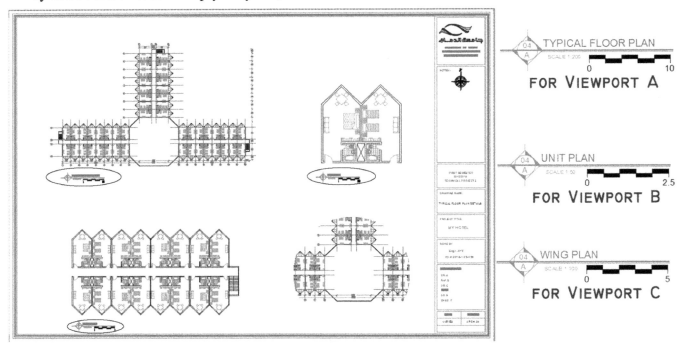

Fig. 7.23 – Show Scale for each Viewport

38. Type PLOT ↵ or Ctrl-P. Plot dialog box appears.
39. Everything is ready. Change Plot style table (pen assignments) if needed. Press OK to get the plot.

Next Step   Building Information Modeling (BIM)

In previous 7 days, you have learnt making 2D drawings with AutoCAD. Next step is to learn making 3D, 4D, 5D Building Information Modeling (BIM).

Autodesk® Revit® is software for BIM. With Revit, you can make Architectural model of a building. From the model, you can get all sheets such as floor plans, elevations, sections, 3D model, 3D section, day-time rendering (with natural lighting), night-time rendering (with artificial lighting), perspective views, walkthrough etc. You can apply materials on walls, floors or other surfaces. You can import an AutoCAD drawing in Revit as an underlay and build 3D model on it. Also you can export plans, elevations, sections etc. from Revit to AutoCAD.

From the Architectural model, you can extract information to make a Structural model. Structural model consists of foundations, columns, beams, slabs etc.

You can add Mechanical, Electrical, Plumbing (MEP) services in the Architectural model,

Look at the following project made by using Revit.

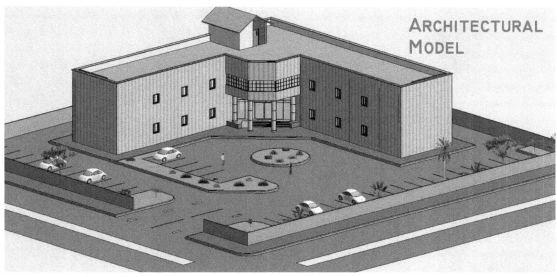

ARCHITECTURAL
MODEL

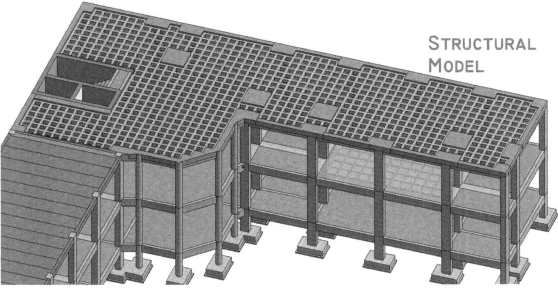

STRUCTURAL
MODEL

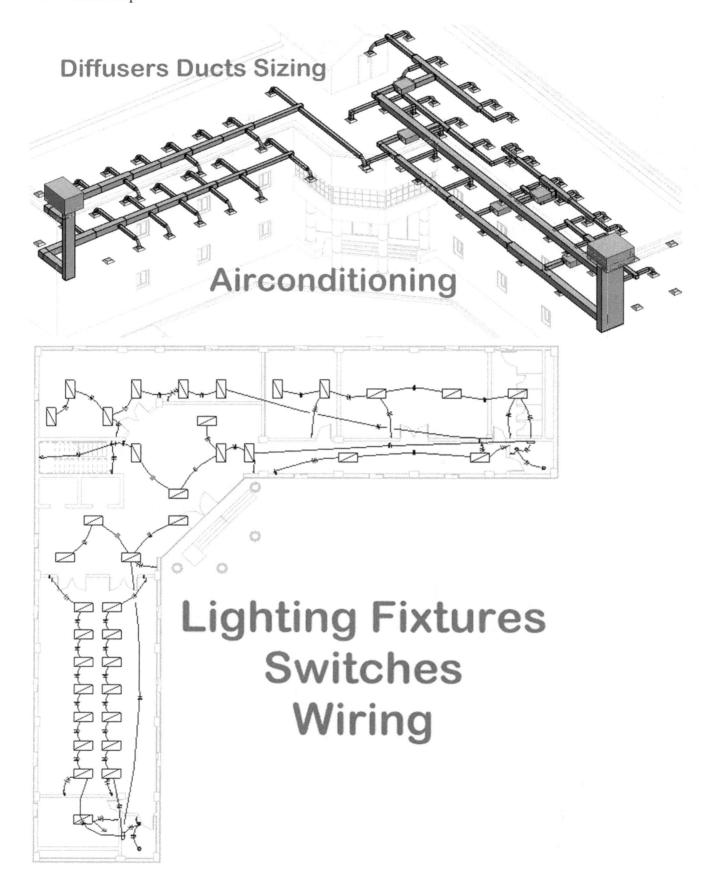

Diffusers Ducts Sizing

Airconditioning

Lighting Fixtures
Switches
Wiring

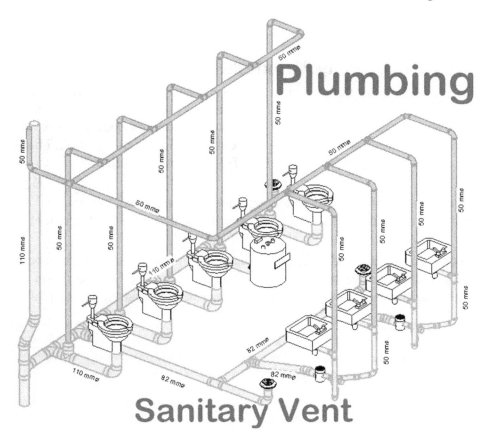

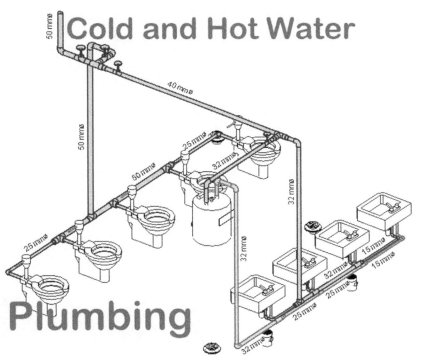

Do you want to make the above Revit project by yourself?

To learn all of this, read the book

Complete Technical BIM Project using Autodesk® Revit®

Suppose you want to make architectural, structural, mechanical, electrical and plumbing models of a building using Autodesk Revit but you don't have any practical experience of using Revit, then this book is for you. You will start from scratch and the book will guide you in step by step procedures to develop the models. I have tried to include all the information needed to develop the models in the book. I hope you will not be stuck at any point and waste your time in searching Help, Internet or other books to work on the topics.

The book doesn't teach you lessons to remember or doesn't ask you questions to answer. From Chapter 1, you start your model and by the end of each chapter, you will see that a part of the model is complete.

The book has three parts: Architecture, Structure and MEP. You start with making architectural model. When it is complete, you will use it to extract information for Structural model. In the last part, you will add services (air-conditioning, lighting, electrical and plumbing) to your architectural model (used as linked model).

Download Table of Contents and first 2 chapters from
http://www.keepandshare.com/doc20/show.php?i=2635007&cat=2

Get the book from https://www.createspace.com/5844227

Watch video at https://www.youtube.com/watch?v=wpiqViiF950

www.ingramcontent.com/pod-product-compliance
Lightning Source LLC
Chambersburg PA
CBHW060450060326
40689CB00020B/4486